"Mary Jo Leddy's pursuit of the ⬛⬛⬛⬛ l
her to some revealing and provol ⬛⬛⬛⬛
   "This book will raise a lot of t. ⬛⬛⬛⬛ f
consternation—all of which we badly need if reiigious ... . ʋe
authentic."

S. Joan Chittister, O.S.B.

"Sister Mary Jo Leddy has made a major contribution to the church, and to religious communities of women particularly, by writing this book. It took courage to write with such honesty and it will take courage to read it. She probes deeply to discover reasons for the severe decline in religious life. But she also provides the beginnings of the 'reweaving' process that could bring a new depth of renewal to religious life and to the whole church."

Thomas J. Gumbleton
Auxiliary Bishop of Detroit

"I read this work with considerable gratitude—it touches a nerve in a community like ours, where we muddle along, rattling, letting go, making do, not many clues, not much light on the next step. It's a courageous, helpful book."

Daniel Berrigan, S.J.

"This reflective essay will be helpful to anyone who is interested in examining how religious life is related to social movements and who, having reached a crossroad, is seeking good advice in preparing to set out in a new direction.

"...a 'must book' on the reading agenda of those involved in renewal of religious life in the Catholic church....Everyone concerned about effective social change will find this book an important reference not only to read now, but to keep on the reference shelf for future consultation."

Marie Augusta Neal
author of *From Nuns to Sisters*

"This is a book of great range and vision as well as concrete practical wisdom. The question it raises is how we might radicalize the vowed life of following the Gospel Christ in the context of a 'pluralistic, bureaucratic' society in contemporary religious life. It is really a spirituality of liberation for North American religious communities.

"It combines a strong literary sense and an easy appropriation of the Scriptures. There is an honest integrity in its concreteness, discussing the ways religious communities try to integrate new members or try to respond to the undeniable 'unraveling' of religious life. This sustained metaphor is brilliant.

"Its strongest mark is its willingness to be self-critical, a rare quality in religious life. It is also strong in its immediacy—integrating personal spiritual journeys, first-hand experiences of communities attempting renewal corporately, and encounters with various models of community life.

"It is a much needed book for our time, especially for those communities of men and women who, having gone through the struggles of renewal, are willing to ask questions about and open themselves to more radical reform."

John Kavanaugh, S.J.
Author of *Following Christ in a Consumer Society*

REWEAVING RELIGIOUS LIFE

Beyond The Liberal Model

Mary Jo Leddy

XXIII
TWENTY-THIRD PUBLICATIONS
Mystic, Connecticut

The poem "Indian Tapestry" by Julia Esquivel is taken from
Threatened With Resurection (Elgin, Ill.: Brethren Press, 1982).
Reprinted with permission.

Twenty-Third Publications
185 Willow Street
P.O. Box 180
Mystic, CT 06355
(203) 536-2611

ISBN 0-89622-440-6
Library of Congress Catalog Card No 90-70354

In Memory of

Kieran Flynn R.S.M.

and

Henry Carr C.S.B.

ACKNOWLEDGMENTS

Although the actual writing of this book was carried out in solitude, it would not have been possible without an ongoing interaction with many persons and groups. It is a joy for me to acknowledge their contributions.

I am grateful to those who took the time to read the early drafts and who offered many valuable suggestions: Helen Marie Burns R.S.M., Margaret Brennan I.H.M., Carol Rittner R.S.M., Mary Ann Hinsdale I.H.M., Constance FitzGerald O.C.D., John Kavanaugh S.J., Michael McGarry C.S.P., Raandi King of Madonna House and Pauline Maheux O.S.U.

Several communities inspired and challenged me in the course of writing this book. The provincial teams of the Religious of the Sacred Heart (in Canada and the United States) were the first groups to invite me to reflect on the situation of religious life in North America. Their encouragement provided the initial impetus toward putting some of my reflections on paper. These reflections were refined through interaction with numerous religious congregations in North America.

The team at Our Lady of Peace Spiritual Life Center in Narragansett, Rhode Island, offered a space of welcome during the summer of 1987 when I attempted a rough draft of this book. The Sisters of Sion in Winnipeg and on Oakmount Road in Toronto and the Ursulines of Chatham (Genesis Community) were constant signs of the promise of religious life.

I want to thank Marge Denis for introducing me to the image of weaving as a way of life. Jennifer Leddy long ago gave me a living sense of what it means to be a "sister." Odilie Solis was a true companion on the pilgrimage described in Chapter Four. Janet Somerville, my associate at *Catholic New Times*, brought her fine sensibility to bear on the first draft of this text. Jack Costello S.J. believed in this book, and in me, far more than I did at times. I am grateful for his fidelity and friendship.

Stephen Scharper of Twenty-Third Publications and my agent, Lee Davis Creal, were most helpful in the process of ensuring the publication of this book.

Finally, I acknowledge the significant support of Frances Ryan O.S.U. Her clear and courageous commitment to religious life has sustained my own commitment to try to see religious life through to the future.

CONTENTS

I watch in admiration
at what comes forth from her mind:
a thousand designs being created and not a single model from
which to copy
the marvellous cloth
with which she will dress
the companion of the True and Faithful One.

Men always ask me
to give the name of the label,
to specify the maker of the design.
But the Weaver cannot be pinned down
by designs,
nor patterns.

All of her weavings
are originals,
there are no repeated patterns.
Her mind is beyond
all foresight.
Her able hands do not accept
patterns or models.
Whatever comes forth, comes forth,
but she who is will make it.

from "Indian Tapestry" by Julia Esquivel

INTRODUCTION

A new book appeared on the shelf of our novitiate library in the fall of 1963: *The Nun in the World*. It seemed rather strange to me at the time, and since I had just made the decision "to leave the world" forever, I wondered what the title could mean.

I sensed, even then, that it meant all the difference in the world.

Those of us who entered religious life in the early 1960s would be the first generation formed almost entirely by the vision of Vatican II. Although I had entered a traditional form of religious life, within months I found myself taking up the challenge Cardinal Suenens had articulated in his small book *The Nun in the World*. In the years that followed, much of my time and energy was engaged in the process of shaping a more liberal model of religious life. With many other religious women, I experienced the profound joys and the real suffering involved in the struggle to renew our way of life.

More recently, my perspective on the liberal model of religious life has begun to shift. I no longer see it as an ideal but simply as a very important phase in the development of religious life. Because this liberal model is the predominant mode of religious life in North America, I suggest that the future of religious life on this continent (and perhaps elsewhere) will depend on our willingness to explore the possibilities and limitations of this model—in the hope of moving beyond it.[1]

This is the thread of thought that will be followed throughout *Reweaving Religious Life: Beyond the Liberal Model* in an effort to contribute to the future of religious life in North America. I discovered this thread of thought in the interweaving of various experiences since the time of Vatican II. It emerged slowly as a tensile truth, at the frayed edges of my work as an editor of an independent Catholic newspaper, of my involvement in various justice and peace issues, and of my service as a resource person for several religious congregations in the United States and Canada. I began to follow this thread of thought on the run and by the way until I had the time and space to gather it into the loom of my own soul and to test its connecting truth.

This book is an attempt both to criticize the predominant model of religious life in North America and to encourage the creation of a new, post-liberal model. My desire to be at once critical and constructive flows from my conviction of the importance of religious life as a prophetic gift for the church. My critique is as strong as my hope in the promise of religious life for the world and for the church.

It has not been easy to sustain this critique because it has also involved self-criticism, including much of the way I have lived my religious life. This criticism has been made even more difficult by my awareness of the criticisms the Vatican has leveled at the liberal tendencies in the church and religious life in North America. The effort of some Vatican officials to make the "L-word" a bad word is patently self-serving. One hesitates to open the door of self-criticism when there are conservatives ready to batter down any structure in the church that shelters liberalism.

However, I know from my experience in working on justice issues that there is also a risk in reacting by defending what is under attack. This dynamic has led to the demise of many groups working for social change. These groups, which have developed a rather sophisticated analysis of many issues, inevitably begin to experience pressure and criticism. Feeling beseiged, they become even more critical of the forces that have attacked them and in the process lose the ability to examine their own analyses and strategies. A rigidity of thought and action sets in, which makes these groups incapable of responding to changes in circumstances and events.

Thus, even though the self-criticism of religious seems problematic, it has never been more necessary. Our future will be as real as our commitment to a realistic assessment of our present situation. Those of us who have been involved in the process of liberalizing religious life are more likely to know its real limitations than any Vatican official. Similarly, those who have been engaged in the process of social change in this culture are more likely to understand the dark underside of liberalism than those who have attempted to stand above it all. To admit that there are problems with the liberal model of religious life is not to assume that this is the personal problem of those who are living this way of life. It does presume that this is a cultural problem and that the crisis in the liberal model of religious life reflects the wider and deeper problem of liberalism in the West.

Yet, when all is said and done, it is far easier to critique the present than to create an alternate future—especially if we believe that such a future is not only our work but also God's gift. We are living through one of those historical in-between times when a former model of religious life (either traditional or liberal) is fading away and a future model has not yet become clear. One could be tempted to flee from the dilemmas of this moment to some more secure past, to the surface of the present, or to some arbitrary resolution of the future. These are real temptations and they can be met only with the faith that this is our hour, our "kairos." This is the only time and place we are called to become followers of Jesus Christ; there is no better time or place for us to live out the mysteries of creation, incarnation, and redemption. These are our times and, in the end, God's time. This is why we can say with Julian of Norwich, who lived in a very dark historical moment, "All shall be well, and all shall be well, and all manner of things shall be well."

In pondering the location of religious life in this in-between time, I have searched for an image to describe the kind of response that will help to create a new and, as yet, unknown model of religious life. This image was a long time in coming. The many images that have been used to describe a relationship to the future fall into one of two extremes: some imagine the process of discerning a *picture* of the future, which will then focus our present efforts; others imagine that going with the *process*, the flow of the present, will cast us upon the shore of the future. One set of images reveals our desire to control the future and the other set, our tendency to abdicate the responsibility for choosing the future.

What image, I wondered, reveals the particular combination of activity and receptivity that is involved in shaping the future during this in-between time?

That image presented itself to me as I was watching a friend weaving a scarf on a loom with the wool she had unraveled from an old sweater. She had no pattern to follow and yet she was doing something; she was making something new. The image of weaving suggested the kind of activity that can take place within a certain framework, even in the absence of any clear pattern. The fact that my friend was reweaving strands of material that had previously been woven into another shape provided an even fuller image of the call of religious during this dangerous and delicate in-between time. Thus, the title of this book and the extended metaphor that will be drawn out in the following chapters.

Reweaving Religious Life begins with a tenuous thread of thought: that the fabric of religious life in North America is unraveling. In its conservative or liberal modes, it is coming apart at the seams. Chapter One explores the intuition that the fabric of American society itself has become frayed and worn out. In this chapter, I attempt to present a thoughtful feel for "The Texture of the Times" by drawing out some of the reasons (suggested by various writers) for seeing this period in history as the time of the decline of the American empire. To identify ourselves, Americans and Canadians, as citizens of an empire may be a disconcerting thought. It may be disorienting to consider that our political system is in a process of decline. Yet, such a perspective may serve to locate the real vocation of religious in this time and in this place. Even if such thoughts leave us at loose ends, they are a necessary consideration in the process of discovering which threads of our culture have become too worn to be helpful in the process of reweaving religious life.

Chapter Two traces some of the subtle consequences of the genuine efforts of religious to become more connected with the fabric of this culture. To the extent that religious congregations after Vatican II became more tied to this broader social fabric, they gradually internalized the patterns of disintegration found within the American empire. Thus, "The Unraveling of Religious Life."

This is not to deny that there are strands within American culture and history that may continue to sustain an authentic religious response for the sake of the Kingdom. However, it is to suggest that there are some ties to the American empire that may have become ties that bind. These ties are a form of bondage that must be cast off in the process of reweaving religious life.

Such considerations invite us to be with the reality of "This Threadbare Moment" in religious life. Chapter Three is an in-between chapter about this in-between moment in which the past lies in tatters and the future has yet to be formed. In such a moment, a choice must be made about how to engage ourselves in the present so that the future may emerge. We can choose, on the one hand, to try to fabricate a future through various projects and projections. On the other hand, we can engage in the task of reweaving religious life. There is a world of difference between these two options: the one fosters illusions and the other nourishes hope.

Reweaving involves selecting those strands of the Spirit, which are to be found among the shreds of religious life and in the texture of the culture, that can sustain a new fabric for the future. The process of reweaving these strands together is a multidimensional activity involving the hands of our hearts, the seeing of our souls.

Chapter Four describes the process of discerning which "Strands of the Spirit," within the tradition of the church and within the culture, can be helpful in reweaving religious life. Such a discernment is necessarily tentative and it is my hope that it will serve to encourage others to begin to distinguish between the ties that bind us to the empire and those strands of the Spirit in North America that connect us with the Kingdom, which is growing among us even now.

The final chapter of this book will discuss the activity of "Reweaving Religious Life" as a process involving both commitment and consciousness. While the previous chapters explore *why* revitalizing religious life is urgent and *where* that process may begin to take place, this chapter examines the *when* and *how* and *by whom*. I will explore the process of revitalizing existing religious congregations as counter-cultural communities. This moment in history will probably call forth in the church new charisms and new communities. It may also invite established congregations to a new charismatic moment.

Throughout these chapters, there is a shift in the mode of discourse. The first two chapters have been written in a more critical mode of reflection. The middle chapter invites the reader into a more contemplative mode, and the final two chapters attempt to evoke the kind of creative reflection and action that will open up the future of religious life. Critical analysis, contemplative presence, and creative action are all ways of being that are called for at this moment. Although readers may find themselves drawn to one way of being or one mode of reflection, my hope is that they will grow in a deeper appreciation of all the dimensions involved in reweaving religious life.

I have attempted to communicate these reflections on religious life for educated although not necessarily academic readers. Those who wish to pursue certain points may want to refer to the notes of each chapter.

In the course of writing this book over a period of two years, I became aware that there were others who were asking some of the same questions and answering them in different but related ways: Joan Chittister O.S.B., Michael Crosby O.F.M. Cap., and Gerald Arbuckle S.M. This was an exciting discovery for me, since it suggests that there is something "in the air." It made me recall a talk in which Gustavo Gutiérrez described his own role in the development of liberation theology. "I didn't create liberation theology," he said. "It was in the air. All it needed was a name." Something new is happening in religious life in North America and it is beginning to find a name.

It should be obvious by now that these reflections begin by examining religious life within the context of culture and then proceed to discussing religious life within the context of church. This is a different line of thought—different, for example, from beginning by reflecting on religious life within the church and then moving to situate it within the culture. Many writers have begun their reflections from within the ecclesial context and their writings have contributed enormously to articulating the promise and problems of post-Vatican II religious life. Yet, it seems equally helpful to begin by reflecting on the cultural context of religious life. This is a different starting point and one which, I would suggest, reveals a different set of problems and possibilities for religious life.

Many metaphors flow from the central metaphor of reweaving religious life, as will become more evident in the following pages. Like every metaphor, it has its limits, but it also opens up new insights. More to the point, it has the potential for liberating prayer and action which is inspired by an engagement in the reality of our time.

Let me acknowledge, at the outset, some of the ways in which my reflections arise from my own experiences as a committed apostolic religious, as a Canadian, and as a woman. It is my conviction that this should help, rather than hinder, others to find their own ground and to take their own stance in life.

Obviously, I have written this book out of my particular way of becoming more Christian: as a member of a religious congregation. It is from within this commitment that my life is woven and rewoven; here I weave and reweave. However, I believe it is important for everyone in the church that religious congregations embody the prophetic response that was called forth at the time of their origins. The authentic strengthening of one vocational strand within the church can only strengthen other vocations within it. I have not attempted to speak for those who have other commitments in the church. My hope is that my search through the texture of these times will encourage other Catholics and other Christians to weave their own response in the midst of the disintegration of the American empire. If I have deliberately avoided drawing out conclusions for other Catholics (clergy or lay) or for members of other Christian denominations, it is because of my respect for the uniqueness of the various gifts within the church. The particular vocations within the ecclesial community are unique threads of grace that must be rewoven in a particular way. Ultimately, we are all being rewoven on the same loom of the Spirit. It is my conviction that this is not the time to fashion a definitive theology about the various roles and ministries within the church. This is not the time to knot each theological thread. It is a time to see through each vocational thread within the church until it reaches a point where it becomes woven with other strands of the Spirit.

Nevertheless, this book may be helpful to any group trying to live the reality of an in-between moment, between its past definitions and the still-to-be-determined future. The spirituality of such a moment is something we are all invited to deepen.

I write as a Canadian, as a citizen of a country that has always been a colony of some empire: first of France, then of England, and now of the United States. We Canadians are so thoroughly colonized that we find it difficult to stand our own ground and to name our own place. Through my involvement with *Catholic New Times*, an independent national newspaper, I have been part of a small but significant effort to articulate a theology that is truly located in the Canadian experience. In the process, I have discovered that living in a colony can sometimes give you an important perspective on life in the heart of the empire. I have written extensively on the difference between the Canadian and American experiences and on how that difference has shaped past history and present responses of religious communities in these two countries.[2]

Nevertheless, it remains true that Canadians are part of the American empire and, willingly or unwillingly, are part of the process of its historical decline. We too live behind the plastic curtain of the consumer culture. We too have inherited the tradition of Western liberal capitalism. While there are significant differences between religious life as it has evolved in the United States and in Canada, there are also some profound similarities.

For the past 15 years I have moved between Canada and the United States. Through my work with Pax Christi USA, with the *National Catholic Reporter*, with several American religious communities, with the Leadership Conference of Women Religious, and in the course of teaching in American academic institutions, I have come to respect the greatness of the founding vision of the republic. My American friends have taught me that some of the best critics of the empire are those whose commitment to the founding ideals of the republic is as strong as their commitment to the Reign of God. Dangerous memories of the republic and the Reign of God lie at the heart of a hope that religious life can flourish anew even in the midst of a declining empire.

Throughout this book, I have used the rather awkward term "religious life in North America" to describe our shared experience of the crisis of the American empire. I suspect that this articulation of a shared sense of crisis will find an echo in other industrialized countries which are experiencing the general decline of the West.

Finally, it should be evident that the central metaphor that shapes this book, weaving, is a feminine metaphor. Indeed, my reflections are shaped by my experience as a woman, in a women's community in the church.[3] This experience is, thereby, as promising as it is problematic. I have no doubt that the emerging feminist consciousness in women's congregations will be essential in the creation of a promising future in religious life. But I am also convinced that this promise will be realized only to the extent that feminism can free itself from an identification with the patterns of liberalism in this culture. Although some of what I write will apply only to women's communities, my sense is that my basic questions and hopes for the future of religious life will be shared by those men in religious communities who want to take their cultural context seriously.

Because this book is part of the process of reweaving religious life, it remains essentially an unfinished product. There are many loose ends I have not attempted to tie up neatly or quickly. In these threadbare times, it seems more important to draw out any insight, any thread of hope, however slender, that connects us on the loom of life.

"We have no vision, no models
or metaphors to live by."
Denys Arcand

"Undoubtedly something is about to happen.
Or is it that something has stopped happening?"
Walker Percy

"As winter completes an age,
The eyes huddle like cattle, doubt
Seeps into the pores and power
Ebbs from the heavy signet ring."
W.H. Auden

"Everybody knows the boat is leaking."
Leonard Cohen

CHAPTER ONE

THE TEXTURE OF THE TIMES

Religious life has always been shaped by a profound realization of the mystery of God and by some evaluation of the reality of the times. Throughout the ages, God has walked among us as the Christ and has exercised a real and absolute claim on the lives of human beings. Today, as yesterday and tomorrow, Jesus attracts men and women, inviting them to follow him. We know from history and from our own experience that this is so. We know that such an invitation evokes the desire to respond with the whole of one's life for all of one's life. Yet, how this response takes concrete shape depends not only upon our personal "timing" but also upon a general assessment of the world and times we live in.

A CRITICAL CONNECTION

It makes a difference if we see the world about us as promising or problematic, as closer to heaven or nearer to hell. This difference of perspectives has, in the past, given rise to various views of the mission of the church and has called forth diverse models of religious life.

In the last thirty years or so, we have seen in the church and in religious life three significant evaluations of the state of the world we live in: the conservative, the liberal, and the radical assessments of contemporary culture.

Rejecting the World

The conservative, or traditional, model of religious life was based on a clear judgment that the modern world, which had been heralded by the Enlightenment, was a place of peril for the faith. As a consequence, religious life (within the well-defended fortress of the church) developed a spirituality and practice that would keep it clearly separated from the modern world. The belief that God was separate from the vicissitudes of the world coincided with the separation of religious from the world. Men and women "left the world" and lived in a cloister, assuming different names, wearing different clothes, and following a different schedule from their brothers and sisters who were involved in more "mundane" activities such as raising a family and earning a living.

This more traditional way of religious life has been much caricatured in various films and plays. There are those who view it, in retrospect, as either quaint or queer. Some are fascinated by the mysterious otherness of it all, while others are suspicious of a way of life that was never lived out in the open. Unfortunately, this was and is how the more traditional model of religious life was often viewed from those outside its reality.

Yet, as many within the church and within religious congregations know, the essential truth of this traditional form of religious life was far more than any of the caricatures of it. It was a coherent way of life in which every dimension of life was ordered by a common vision and by a shared system of meaning and symbols. It was a way of life capable of commanding greatness of heart, sacrifice, and commitment. It was also susceptible to pettiness of spirit and the trivial pursuits of piety. The old days of religious life were not always good but they were sometimes great. Throughout North America, schools and hospitals and various social services were born out of nothing but the love and generosity of countless men and women who gave their lives within religious congregations. In responding to needs that were as yet unmet, religious were animated by a sense of purpose and vision. I recall conversations with the older members of my own congregation and their descriptions of the many sacrifices that were necessary to help build a new school. They recall those days as the happiest of their lives. United in a common commitment, they willingly assumed the discipline and deprivations demanded by this commitment. There was an abundance of charity and joy and, so they say, more than a measure of peace.

Obviously, apostolic religious congregations were founded for the service of those in the world. Yet, it must be said that they were not involved directly in the world. Religious met and served others on a kind of middle ground, usually Catholic institutions. Thus, people from the world would go to a Catholic school or hospital where the structure was shaped by the values of a religious congregation. In other words, religious set the terms for their encounter with the world. The traditional model of religious life was part of the subculture of Catholicism on this continent. One could even say that it was, in its own way, counter-cultural.

Relevant to the World
The Second Vatican Council (1962–1965) was an historic turning point for all groups within the Roman Catholic church. This amazing convocation of the Spirit opened itself to the intuition that the church should become a participant in the modern world. This intuition germinated in Europe in the decade before the council, but it was a seed that took root quickly in the responsive soil of North America. As some have observed, even if Vatican II had not happened, American Catholics in the early 1960s would have developed a confident maturity that would have prepared them to move beyond the ghetto Catholicism that had nurtured their faith and identity throughout their immigrant experience.[1] The church, which had become a stronghold against the modern world, lowered its drawbridge and, as the people of God, crossed over into the twentieth century. The church took this risk because it knew it had become so separated from the world as to become almost irrelevant. Unless the church became more "relevant," so

many of the council fathers said, it risked becoming entombed in its own structures while the life of the world went on without it.

"Relevance" became a new code word in the church, and it was thus that Cardinal Suenens of Belgium wrote the little book, *The Nun in the World,* that would find its way to the library of a small novitiate on the prairie of western Canada. Most of the novices who read it could barely pronounce "ecumenical," the word used to describe the important meeting that had been going on in Rome. What is astounding, in retrospect, is that we and many religious in North America took the words of Vatican II so seriously. The council documents were far more than material for spiritual reading; they set an agenda for action.

Many religious congregations, which had been largely disconnected from the world, moved quickly to make those changes that would allow them to connect with contemporary society. We moved out of the coherent subculture of religious life and into the chaotic culture of North America. It was not a mindless move; it had an impressive theoretical impetus from theologians such as Karl Rahner, who had rearticulated the relationship between God and the world, between grace and nature. He argued against the theology that would separate God from the world. By implication, he said that religion should not be confined to certain special times (such as Sunday) or to certain special places (such as a church or a convent) or to certain special people (such as priests and religious). Rather, God was the mysterious and ultimate center of all of life. Religion and thereby religious life were to be discovered and lived in the midst of the world.

The move of religious into the world was momentous—for themselves and for those associated with them. Many religious recall the anxieties of that time associated with the move out of enclosed spaces, habitual ways of dressing, and defined modes of service. We no longer set the terms for meeting the world. Within religious congregations, it was a time of nervous excitement. No other group within the church (at least in the United States and Canada) experienced so intimately the joys and sufferings involved in taking Vatican II seriously. This was particularly true for women religious who, unlike their brothers in religious life, did not have the relative security of clerical identity to fall back on.

Future historians may puzzle over how quickly we were willing to let go of an entire, coherent way of life. They would have to understand that the more traditional model of religious life was a beautiful fruit that had become overripe and was ready to fall. They would have to study the whole socio-economic context of Europe and North America in the 1950s and early 1960s. It seems clear, even now, that the optimistic view of the world articulated at Vatican II was greatly influenced by the cheerful prosperity of the middle class in Europe in the 1950s. This mood was easily shared by confident North American Catholics in the early 1960s. For these Catholics, who had emerged victorious from the Second World War, the times seemed more full of promise than of peril. The world was developing and progressing and Catholics wanted to be part of it, not separated from it. Future historians would have to situate the willingness of religious to re-enter the world within the context of the cultural optimisim in the United States and Canada during the early 1960s. The election of John F. Kennedy in the United States seemed to embody all things bright and beautiful—and he was Catholic. In Canada, the celebration of Expo 67 and the election of the dazzling Pierre Trudeau as Prime Minister seemed to assure a new and "just" society.

Few of us at the time were conscious of the fact that we were entering a world shaped by the values of liberalism. Even those who were conscious of this felt that these values were good and much needed in the church. Gregory Baum, an influential theologian during the Second Vatican Council, tells the story of his encounter with a young Italian communist at the time in Rome. Baum was explaining his enthusiasm for all the changes in the conservative way of doing theology. The young Italian remarked, with some disdain, that it was all "so liberal." This was rather confusing for Baum at the time, since he thought that "liberal" could only mean something positive.

For many post-Vatican II Catholics, "liberal" was used to describe any positive change from the more traditional ways of being church. If the traditional church was hierarchical, uniform, and authoritarian, the liberal church would be communitarian, pluralistic, and tolerant. The liberal church would attempt to be more reflective of, and more relevant to, the culture.

This rather flattering assessment of the culture led many religious congregations to criticize their own structures and, indeed, the structures of the church. God only knows the time and energy that went into trying to change various structures to allow for more personal freedom, wider pluralism of expression, and a greater tolerance for diversity. Many women and men left religious life at this time either because of negative experiences in the traditional model of religious life or because they had arrived at some positive sense of another personal direction.

The Way of Resistance
However, this optimistic assessment of our culture began to change slowly but significantly during the mid-1970s and 1980s. Those religious who continued to take seriously the Vatican II imperative to "read the signs of the times" noticed that the signals were becoming more mixed. Those who had become more than superficially involved in the world experienced it as a place that could not only reveal but also conceal the action of the Spirit. Dramatic socio-economic changes in North America began to move some religious to see the underside of their own culture. The Vietnam War was the first major crack in the once solid wall of unquestioning American patriotism. Then, too, there were those who began to share the perspective of their brothers and sisters in the third world and see the world through the eyes of the poor. Missionaries who had flown off to the third world, in response to Pope Paul VI's call, came home to roost. They had seen how the American dream had become a nightmare for many in other places in the world. They told stories about what they had seen and heard. The Berrigan brothers, Daniel and Philip, and many others in the peace movement began to expose the idolatrous dependency of the West on nuclear arms.

This is the third assessment of our relationship to the world—the radical. Beyond the desire to be relevant, some religious are searching for a way of life to sustain an authentic resistance to the world. This resistance is different from the way of rejection of the world that characterized the more traditional model of religious life; it bears little resemblance to the option for relevance that has animated the liberal model. Unlike the conservative model of religious life, the way of resistance is connected to the world. Unlike the liberal model, which is well connected to the world, the radical model of resistance is *critically connected* to the culture.

Yet, it must be said that this more radical, post-liberal model of religious life is not characteristic of religious congregations in North America. It would be more accurate to say that all three models of religious life—conservative, liberal, and radical—co-exist somewhat tensely within most congregations. The existence of this plurality of models indicates the extent to which most religious communities are operating out of a liberal value system of diversity and tolerance. Whether this pluralism should be or even can be sustained—and for how long—is one of the crucial, and largely unarticulated, questions facing religious congregations today. I suggest that we cannot even begin to ask (much less to answer) this question until we examine the texture of our times even more closely.

SEEING THROUGH

Developing critical consciousness, examining the texture of the times, has been taken seriously by those church groups involved in the process of social change. They have developed various approaches, each with distinctive ways and means and words. Yet, these groups are animated by a common awareness that the world is not as it could or should be. The development of a class consciousness, a feminist consciousness, an ecological consciousness, an ethnic consciousness, etc., is seen as crucial in moving oneself and others beyond the usual acceptance of "the way things are." The political implications of critical consciousness are significant, and the philosophical questions involved in this process are substantial, such as the relationship between theory and practice, knowledge and human interests. Any sustained effort to relate to the texture of the times inevitably involves us in the question of the relationship between consciousness and commitment.

People approach this relationship with different emphases. Some stress the importance of critical analysis as the basis for liberating action. Others hold that an engagement in concrete situations and a commitment to real people awaken the passion for deeper social analysis. I identify more with this latter group, partly because of my involvement in the peace movement and in trying to educate people about the threat of nuclear weapons. I have seen how massive doses of information about the possibility of a global holocaust seem to leave people more paralyzed than purposeful in action. The more we know, the less we seem able to do. Yet, I have also been with people who want to do more, perhaps because of those they love, perhaps because it is in their self-interest to do so. Since they want to do more, they want to know more and get to the bottom of things. This kind of commitment awakens our courage to develop greater consciousness, to take more risks as we enter the darkness. Committed people are willing to explore the deeper problems, which may call forth an even deeper commitment. Those who are not committed have already decided not to pay the price of greater consciousness. Anyone who has already decided never to lift a sandbag will never be ready to see the flood of coming events.

For these and other reasons, I have found it most helpful to use the term "seeing through" to describe the kind of critical commitment necessary for living faithfully in these times. "Seeing through" has a double meaning; it indicates the double activity required of Christians in the cultural context of North America. We "see through" when we see through the appearances of this historical moment to the deeper, underlying realities of the present. Seeing through also implies "seeing something through," i.e., making present decisions and commitments to carry something forward into the future.

This book is an exercise in this process of "seeing through." The first two chapters are an attempt to see through the relatively superficial problems of this culture (and of religious life in it) to the more fundamental problems that must be addressed. These chapters are an excursion, however preliminary, into darkness and disintegration. The reflections contained in these chapters presume a commitment to see religious life through this particular historical moment. Without such a commitment, there will not be the freedom to explore the depth and extent of the problems we face as North Americans and as religious people. With such a commitment, we will resist the temptation to rush in with easy answers and temporary solutions to our problems. Ultimately, this commitment is sustained by the belief that God is with us in this darkness, seeing us through. Darkness is not dark to God.

I withhold any reflections about the deeper signs of hope, which arise in the course of seeing through the present moment, until the last two chapters. There are indeed signs in North America that can enlighten our hope, but to introduce them prematurely could diffuse the reality of darkness of these times. Much of the grayness in religious life today reflects a denial of the dark threads within our culture and within the fabric of our congregations. This grayness has little to do with the reality of aging membership in religious congregations. It is a state of mind, a state of soul.

Definition Through Description
Although much more could be written in philosophical terms to *define* the process of "seeing through," I have discovered in the course of my work with religious communities that it is more helpful to *describe* this process by referring to my own process of "seeing through" the texture of the times. In practice, the process is much more muddled than one would want. There are lapses of thought and leaps of nerve. One prays as one can—back to the wall, ear to the ground, every hair on one's head counting on Love.

Trying to see through one's culture is like trying to see the nose on your face, for culture is that all-pervasive reality of the symbols, institutions, and systems of meaning that structures not only our society but our inner selves as well. It helps to nose around a bit. My own cultural analysis began to sharpen during the years we lived in a poorer neighborhood in Toronto called Parkdale. I lived there because of my increasing discomfort with speaking about poverty at some remove from persons who were poor.

Living in Parkdale pushed me to see through much of the rhetoric that either reviled or romanticized the poor. I began to see the larger socio-political world through the eyes of the poor, my neighbors. It was not a pretty picture. The shuffling steps of the released mental patients on the streets led me to conclude that, whatever the manipulators of statistics were saying, things were not getting better. These street people carried in their bodies the insight that things were getting worse. Beat up and broken down, they revealed in their flesh all the oversights that politicians and pundits are prone to. Seeing the world through the eyes of the poor helped me to see more clearly; those who lived at the margins of society revealed to me the truth about the core of this society. I learned this simple maxim: where you live determines what you see; whom you listen to determines what you hear.

I began to see how many of my views about life in general and about religious life in particular had been shaped by a kind of economically induced optimism. Before we moved to Parkdale, we had been living in a rather trendy, yuppie area of the city called the Annex. The difference between these two neighborhoods, these two perspectives on life, began to crystallize for me when it began to snow. The sight of the first snow in the Annex was often the occasion for some excited conversation between neighbors about the possibility of going skiing, and remarks about how lovely the block looked all decked out in white. The falling snow in Parkdale, though, felt quite different. For the homeless, the sight of snow aroused feelings of impending dampness and cold. The challenge was not to find a good place to ski, but rather to find a place to sleep and keep warm. Conversations centered around which of the donut shops would be open for 24 hours. Same snow, different angles of vision. From one perspective, life looked lovelier; from another, life became more of a struggle to survive.

Our semi-conscious commitment to live in Parkdale had led to a change in consciousness and perspective, and this had, in turn, given us the courage of our convictions. I found myself publicly criticizing politicians and church leaders who conducted panels on unemployment in five-star hotels that were inaccessible to public transportation. They meant well; they simply didn't realize that not everyone has a car.

During the time I lived in Parkdale, I also worked at *Catholic New Times*—on a shoestring budget. We started this newspaper in 1976 with more commitment than cash. It had been born out of the conviction that we needed to be a voice for the many faith and justice efforts that were taking shape in the church at that time. The difficulties involved in bringing this newspaper to birth and of nurturing its growth were many. Yet, somehow it all seemed worthwhile if we could provide an alternative to the more conservative official Catholic newspaper in Canada.

In the fall of 1986, we decided to review our experiences together and to reflect on the significance of the ten-year period in church history that we had written about and had been so involved in. This retreat together was a salutary time to reflect. The deadlines and the as-it-happens nature of journalism tend to reduce one's perspective to the present moment.

In reflecting on the various issues that we had covered or editorialized on during those ten years, I was struck by the repetitive and even predictable quality of many of the church stories in the newspaper. For every event of significance for Roman Catholics, there was always a predictably different response from the conservatives or liberals in the church. On any particular issue one side approved of an action, and the other side disapproved. It was like watching a see-saw, up and down. Yet, I wondered, is the discussion really going anywhere? Like any see-saw, it was static at its center.

This conflict between liberals and conservatives seemed to parallel the argument going on between these two groups within the broader social context. I realized that this conflict made for easy and colorful journalism. It was all too predictable. Reality is never that predictable. What, I puzzled, is really going on? If my experience in Parkdale had led me to a deeper awareness of something problematic in our society, my work at *Catholic New Times* had pushed me to the intuition that the problems in the church might be connected to some deeper social problems. I was stuck between half-formed questions and failing answers.

Just before the *Catholic New Times'* anniversary retreat, I saw the award-winning film, *The Decline of the American Empire,* by Quebec director Denys Arcand. The first five minutes of that film "named" something I already knew but only in an inchoate fashion.[2] In the opening scene, we hear an articulate and rather jaded academic analyze the present state of affairs to a young radio interviewer. In a time of political decline, says the professor, people cease to invest their energy in a common social project and turn toward more personal projects, such as the development and fulfillment of the self. Only in developing societies, she lectures, is there a common social vision compelling enough to invite individuals to transcend their personal interests for the sake of something greater.

The rest of this film is an exploration of the cultivation of the self which takes place in a group of Montreal academics on a weekend together. The women exercise on Nautilus equipment while the men cook a gourmet meal. Commitments of every kind fall by the wayside on this weekend—all for the sake of more personal pleasure or power. What remains is only a vague sense of belonging to a group of similarly motivated people.

One curious statement floats out unexpectedly near the end of the film: "We have no vision, no models or metaphors to live by. Only the saints and mystics live well in a time like this." (The significance of this statement may become more apparent in Chapter Three.)

The Decline of the American Empire is an example of the way artists often name the reality of a culture before they or we know it in any conceptual or analytic form. Between the facts of our social experience and any theological reflection on them, we need the mediating images of artists and storytellers to give us some way of seeing through the texture of our times. Denys Arcand provided me with a name for the historico-cultural reality shaping the church and religious life here and now. Our time, he suggests, is the time of "the decline of the American empire."

The Decline of the American Empire
Whether we know it or not, those of us who live in the Western

world are going through a massive shift in historical consciousness: from a consciousness of being part of a well-developed
world to an inchoate awareness of being part of a declining culture. This shift in consciousness makes all the difference in the
world and is of crucial significance for religious life. Periods of
shifts in historical consciousness have always been occasions of a
shift in the model of religious life, e.g., the founding of new communities or the revitalization of existing congregations. These
were also times when some congregations ceased to exist or
moved into a survival pattern. Such a shift in historical consciousness is difficult and demanding.

It is not easy to entertain the thought that we are living in an
"empire." The word conjures up images of exploitation, which
seem to conflict with our stated political values of freedom, justice, and tolerance. Yet, every now and then someone speaks,
more in sorrow than in anger, about the widening gap between
our political ideal and the reality of the empire. I vividly recall
Congresswoman Patricia Schroeder speaking at a hastily arranged press conference on behalf of some members of the Leadership Conference of Women Religious who had been stopped
from entering Honduras in January 1985. We had flown to Honduras in the hope of holding a prayer vigil at one of the American
military installations on the Honduran-Nicaraguan border. Our
plane had been stopped on the tarmack in Tegucigalpa and
boarded by armed guards who ordered us back to Miami.

Surrounded by the returned women religious, Schroeder said,
"This government has taken the torch of freedom from the Statue
of Liberty and has replaced it with an M-16 rifle. This is the image
of America that others see." Then she looked around at the wom-
en who had just gotten off the plane and said, "But that is not
America; America is here, here in this room."

Another woman eloquently expressed a similar point of view
on the occasion of the bicentennial celebration in 1976. Philosopher
Hannah Arendt, who had written (in 1963) a passionate philosophical argument supporting the founding ideals of her adopted
country, now lamented that these ideals had become more image
than reality by the time of the Vietnam war.

Among the many unprecedented events of this century the swift decline in power of the United States should be given due consideration.

We may very well stand at one of those decisive turning points of history which separate whole eras from each other. For contemporaries entangled, as we are, in the inexorable demands of daily life, the dividing lines between eras may be hardly visible when they are crossed; only after people stumble over them do the lines grow into walls which irretrievably shut off the past....

The American institutions of liberty, founded two hundred years ago, have survived longer than any comparable glories in history. These highlights of man's historical record have rightfully become the paradigmatic models of our tradition of political thought; but we should not forget that, chronologically speaking, they were always exceptions. As such they survive splendidly in thought to illuminate the thinking and doing of men in darker times....

People are aware of the fearful distance that separates us from our extraordinary beginnings.[3]

It is equally uncomfortable to think of ourselves as living in a time of historical decline. We are so accustomed to thinking of North America as, more or less, in a process of ongoing development. We, Americans and Canadians, see ourselves as living in the "developed world" and we tend to refer to other countries to the south as being part of the "underdeveloped world." What a sea change it would be for us to begin to think of ourselves as part of an overdeveloped or even declining nation!

One does not need to be exhaustively informed to have some sense that a significant shift in economic and political power is taking place in the world. The Russian empire has obviously begun to collapse and the fault lines of the American empire are becoming more apparent. We are witnessing the emergence of two new centers of economic power: the new Europe and the Pacific Rim.

I recall watching on television the opening of the 1988 Olympic

Games in Seoul, South Korea, with a group of friends. Everyone was amazed at the sheer display of wealth and talent in the opening program. We wondered if any country could match the facilities that South Korea built. Locating the Olympic Games in the Pacific Rim seemed symbolic of where the competitive energy of the world is shifting.

Once I started to see this period of history as a time of cultural decline, I started to see confirmation of this trend almost everywhere—or so it seemed. It wasn't that this sense of decline had already been articulated and I had been just too blind to notice it. Rather, I was picking up the sense that "something is in the air."

I noticed that the guiding image of Denys Arcand's film was apparent in several recent artistic and literary works. One might question whether these works reflect only a personal sense of diminishment—normal for artists past mid-life—were it not for the growing body of historical, socio-political, and economic studies that provide some amplification of the central insight named by these artists. Some will want to discuss which came first: the artistic image or the analytic studies of the process of decline in America. Suffice it to say that the reality of this time and place is forcing itself into the minds, imaginations, and hearts of a significant number of people in North America. This has been duly noted by the editors of *The New York Times Magazine* who ran an April 1988 cover story entitled "Is America in Decline?"[4] When an image begins to circulate this widely, you know something is in the air.

The notion of the decline of the American empire has found an impressive—and unexpected—spokesman in the person of Yale historian Paul Kennedy. His detailed academic study *The Rise and Fall of the Great Powers* has been a surprising best-seller. Kennedy and three other writers (David P. Calleo of the Johns Hopkins School of Advanced International Studies, Mancur Olson of the University of Maryland, and Walter Russell Mead of *New Perspectives Quarterly*) "represent a new intellectual movement—a School of Decline."[5]

There are a number of other writers, such as Gibson Winter, George Grant, and Joe Holland, who prefer to characterize our present period in history as that of the time of the breakdown of the paradigm that has so dominated Western culture since the Enlightenment. While this broad analysis of the crisis of modernity is important, and I will be referring to some of its implications in the course of this book, there is something significant about specifying this period as the time of the decline of the American empire. Quite simply, this specification brings it all closer to home. It situates our struggles as a church and our questions about religious life in a concrete way. Western civilization today is not an abstraction but a socio-economic and political reality that finds the center of its circumference in one nation, the United States. As England used to be the center of Western civilization in the nineteenth century, so in the twentieth century America has become the center around which nations have circled with only relative degrees of power and independence. Until recently, it was not inaccurate to say that as America goes, so goes the West.

Paul Kennedy proposes that America has now entered a process of decline for the same reasons that led to the fall of other great empires in modern history. His argument rests on the significance of the relationship between economic power and military power. Through a series of historical examples, he documents how political empires enter a stage of decline when the military commitments, deemed necessary to protect the economic investments of the empire, begin to outstrip the empire's economic resources. When this happens, says Kennedy, an empire runs the risk of "imperial overstretch." He holds that a nation's longevity rests on whether it can maintain a balance between the perceived defense requirements and the economic means it possesses to meet those requirements.

Kennedy is quick to emphasize that he is referring to a situation of "relative decline" when speaking of the decline of America. He is not suggesting that America will be reduced to a situation similar to that of many so-called underdeveloped countries. America will continue to be a great power but it will no longer be the center of the world in economic, political, and military terms.

He is saying that, relative to other nations such as the Pacific Rim countries (Japan in particular), America is in a state of economic decline. It is declining, relatively speaking, in terms of productivity and it is increasing its borrowing to the point where it is now the largest debtor nation in the world. Kennedy marshals the statistics to underline the fact that it is America, and not some third world nation, which is the largest debtor nation in the world:

> The continuation of such trends, alarmed voices have pointed out, would push the U.S. national debt to around $13 trillion by the year 2000 (fourteen times that of 1980), and the interest payments on such debt to $1.5 trillion (twenty-nine times that of 1980).[6]

Statistics such as these indicate the extent to which America has lost interest in investing in the future. It was not always thus. Even the greediest of entrepreneurs in turn-of-the century America was trying to get ahead for the sake of his children. He was willing to sacrifice in the present for the sake of his children's future prosperity.

The economic statistics of present-day America are hard facts and Kennedy does not see them being softened by the historical precedents of other empires. As a nation begins to decline, he writes, it is subject to an increasing number of military challenges that force it to allocate even more of its economic resources for defense purposes. This "leads to the downward spiral of slower growth, heavier taxes, deepening domestic splits over spending priorities, and a weakening capacity to bear the burdens of defense."[7]

The point of "imperial overstretch" has serious political as well as economic consequences. There is a point at which the empire's "national security" needs begin to overstretch the limits of democratic procedures and values. "No nation in history has ever managed permanent war and a permanent military Leviathan at its heart and been able to maintain a truly representative character."[8] The Iran-Contra hearings will be noted historically, long after the personalities involved have faded from the scene, for the brief glimpse these hearings provided into how the imperatives of empire threatened to overwhelm the ideal of the democratic process of the republic.

FADING OF THE FUTURE

The thinkers associated with the "school of decline" vary in their estimation of the probable course of America's decline. Historian Kennedy is reluctant to read history according to some organic model which assumes that every new political experiment, like every seed in the ground, is doomed to mature, age, and die. This view of history, he holds, denies the not insignificant factor of human choice and action, which can change the course of history. However, he does see the need to recognize the broad trends that are underway and the need to "manage" the present state of affairs so that the erosion of America's position as "Number One" takes place as smoothly as possible.

Walter Russell Mead seems much more convinced that the process of decline within America is inexorable and irreversible.

He does not attempt a timetable for this process but he does urge us to think clearly about this trend in order to be able to fashion new options within it. "Serious people who are concerned for the well-being of the American people and humanity as a whole need to understand this phenomenon so that they can take appropriate action."[9]

In spite of differing qualifications and nuances, these thinkers are beginning to articulate a major shift in historical consciousness which is taking place within the American empire. In spite of the apparent political victory in the Cold War against communism, America is losing the economic war. "The new order is being created by others and it threatens to lock the United States into long-term economic decline."[10] The future does not look more promising than either the present or the past. The ground is shifting beneath our feet; we might feel the earth trembling but we hardly know what to think about it. For those who have been raised on the American dream of all the possibilities that lie in the future, this dramatic shift in historical consciousness threatens the culturally accumulated sense of identity and purpose.

There is a great deal of denial of and resistance to this shift in historical perspective. Both candidates in the 1988 presidential election, George Bush and Michael Dukakis, knew they had to appeal to the myth of progress which has shaped the identity of America as a nation. One candidate said, "It's morning in America." The other said that "the best of America is yet to come." The denial of the facts of reality is one of the surest signs of the onset of historical decline. It takes a certain faith in the future to wrestle with the realities of the present.

There are other ways in which people begin to cope when they feel the future is more threatening, less compelling or promising. There can be a retreat into the past, not the real past but the past as it should have been but never was. Ronald Reagan was the quintessential representative of such a flight into nostalgia. This kind of trip down memory lane often coincides with an effort to maintain a facade about the future. Again, Ronald Reagan was spellbinding in this regard. He was a living witness to the myth that no one gets old in America, they just get better. Unfortunately, this type of nostalgia prevents us from grounding ourselves in the real past, which is usually better and worse than we would imagine it to be. In any case, it can provide an important basis from which to critique the fads and frenzies of the present. When someone like Ronald Reagan tries to build on the world that never was, the fabrications of the present soon disappear in the harsh light of reality. Gary Wills's description of the ephemeral quality of the comfort offered by nostalgia is brilliant.

> Ronald Reagan did not build a structure; he cast a spell. There was no Reagan revolution, just a Reagan bedazzlement. The magic is going off almost as mysteriously as the spell was woven in the first place. There is no edifice of policies solid enough to tumble, piece by piece, its props being knocked out singly or in groups. The whole thing is not falling down; it was never weighty enough for that. It is simply evanescing.[11]

As a compelling sense of the future fades, some choose to live for the present moment. "Eat, drink and be merry for tomorrow you may perish." While there are only a few subcultures in which the most blatant forms of hedonism are socially acceptable, it remains true that more North Americans than ever prefer to buy now and pay later. Advertising agencies know this and make a direct appeal to the conspicuous consumerism that is in vogue—especially among the young.

Then there are those for whom the diminished sense of a social future becomes associated with the end of the whole world. This apocalyptic view is held by groups as diverse as religious fundamentalists and some anti-nuclear groups. Apocalyptic thinking leads some groups to less social involvement and others to more political action.

Some of the developments within the New Age Movement are indicative of a tendency to flee history entirely when faced with a fading sense of the future. As the external world appears more fragile, there is a cultivation of interiority, or subjectivity, in an effort to reach a "consciousness" that transcends the vicissitudes of a particular time and place. "You work on yourself because there is nothing else. Everything outside is corrupted."[12] The return to the processes of nature and the self has always been characteristic of those periods in history when the political and social processes are breaking down. "Consciousness" becomes the way to connect the processes of nature and the self outside of the forced march or retreat of history. The great romantic poet Johann Goethe acknowledged that the turn toward interiority and subjectivity was characteristic of periods of historical decline in which individuals felt less confident about shaping the external world. "Epochs which are regressive and in the process of dissolution are always subjective, whereas the trend in all progressive epochs is objective."[13]

Some people seem to retain enough culturally induced confidence to believe that they can manufacture, or fabricate, a future through better planning, newer social models, etc. There is something very American (and very Canadian) about believing that if you just work hard enough, just try hard enough, things will get better. At some point, however, this kind of confidence will crash upon the shoals of social reality.

These are all cultural ways of coping with the shift in historical consciousness which is pressing upon our minds and hearts. It is not surprising that some of these ways of coping would be present in religious congregations as they begin to face the uncertainties of their own future. I will say more on this in the following chapter.

It is worth noting that this loss of a sense of the future, which is characteristic of the American empire at this time, has bearing on many of the seemingly disparate social issues of today. Only a very present-centered society, for example, will lay waste the environment and leave it as a garbage heap for future generations. Only such a society will risk a global holocaust in order to preserve its present way of life. There is a dangerous myopia, as I have mentioned above, in mortgaging the future through spending policies in which the benefit to a few now will be paid for by many in the years to come. The contentious question of abortion is another example of an issue that has been cast only in present-centered terms. Often abortion is disputed in terms of the rights of women versus the rights of the unborn. Given the past history of patriarchy, in society and in the church, it is probably inevitable that there will be those who claim that seeing abortion as an issue of womens' rights is an advance. Nevertheless, when we consider (and this is admittedly a gross and partial consideration) that at least half of the unborn are future women, it becomes more difficult to cast abortion simply as an issue of women's rights. It is perhaps more accurate to say that it is an issue of whether the rights and needs of the women and men of this generation will take precedence over the right of the women and men of future generations to take their place in this world.

We struggle, more or less, with these issues. We live, more or less consciously, with the challenge of weighing the imperatives of the present against the fragility of the promises of the future. Often this seems to be a personal dilemma, yet it is a dilemma that uncovers the far greater dilemma of the various political options available to us at the present moment.

THE DISINTEGRATION OF LIBERALISM

The Decline of the American Empire focuses on the difference between living in a society in a state of development and merely existing in a culture in a state of decline. The difference, so the film suggests, has to do with the relative strength or weakness of the common social vision within which an individual lives.

Every social movement or political experiment begins with a vision that animates it and draws it forward. The vision may be stated in the most poetically intuitive images or it may be articulated in a politically refined constitution. In either case, the vision compels the response of those who share in it. A common social vision or ideal is something people aspire to, are exhilarated by, and are willing to make sacrifices for. It transforms present action and interprets it in terms of future possibilities.

The fading of that vision coincides with the dissolution, whether sudden or gradual, of the social movement or socio-political institutions in which it is embodied. The historical precedent of the decline of the Roman empire is pertinent here. Scholars have identified several possible causes of the breakdown of this empire (which took place over several hundred years), and the debate continues as to which of these causes was the key factor. However, this much seems clear: the point at which its military imperialism overstretched its economic limits coincided with the disintegration of the architectonic vision upon which the republic of Rome had been constructed.

America too was founded on a common social vision of a new world of "life, liberty and the pursuit of happiness." It has been a land of dreams, writes Daniel Boorstin, "where the aspirations of people from countries cluttered with rich, cumbersome, aristocratic, ideological pasts can reach for what once seemed unattainable."[14] Can the vision of America, or fragments of it, survive the present socio-economic crisis engendered by political and military "overstretch"?

The effort to cope with the loss of an overarching social vision and an imperative sense of the future takes at least two significant shapes within North America today. To use familiar terms, they can be called the "conservative" and "liberal" political options. Obviously, my description of either of these options must necessarily remain sketchy, since neither conservativism nor liberalism exists as some ideal and unchanging type. Their particular character is modified by many regional and national differences and by the issues that have characterized various periods in North American political history. The conservative tradition in Canada, for example, is quite different from the conservative tradition in the United States. Liberalism tends to be considered more middle-of-the road in Canada than it is in the United States.

Nevertheless, certain characteristics of each of these political options can and should be noted. My purpose in sketching the outlines of these two political options is to suggest how both of them have become ways of coping with the decline of the American empire. These two ways of coping, as I will explain in the next chapter, are also present within most persons and within most religious congregations today.

The conservative effort (on the part of many and diverse groups) is directed toward bringing back some order and meaning in society. Quite simply, conservatives are concerned about the chaos and confusion they perceive in the lives of individuals and society. Thus, their concern about family, morality, and traditional values. The forces of the New Right seem to have a very clear vision of America and its place in the world and they often articulate that vision in the language of religion. Although I do not agree with many of the solutions the New Right has for the problems of America, I do sense that they may well be closer to the heart of the problem than others give them credit for. As Jim Wallis of *Sojourners* magazine has observed, "They [the New Right] have tapped into the deep and legitimate need of the American people for a sense of direction, meaning and commonly held values in public life."[15]

However, it would seem that the conservative effort is doomed to fail for at least two significant reasons. The first has to do with the internal contradictions between the social conservatives (who value the family, etc.) and the economic conservatives (who espouse the unbridled competition of free enterprise). The social consequences of the free-market system are disastrous for traditional social institutions such as the family and religion. The demands of the market have closed down small family businesses, forced people to move away from their extended families and their roots in communities of faith. According to Walter Russell Mead, "The longer and more freely the market operates, the more inexorably it destroys its political base."[16]

The second reason why the conservative effort, in the long run, is doomed to collapse is that a common social meaning and vision cannot be coerced, cannot be imposed. This is particularly true in a democratic society in which such an imposition would corrode the very basis upon which the nation was built. The conservative attempt to impose a common social vision, and thereby bring order into society, will almost always have to rely on the coercive, rather than the creative, use of power.

The coercive use of power is a characteristic of an empire in a state of decline. Ultimately, the conservative way of coping with social decline blinds its adherents to the extent to which they are subtly perpetuating the patterns of decline even as they attempt to come to grips with its disintegrating effects.

In order to understand the limitations of the liberal way of coping with a loss of common social meaning, it is important to examine some of the limitations inherent in its original assumption. Liberalism is based on a philosophy that flowered in the nineteenth century and served to articulate the "beliefs" of the emerging economic order of industrial capitalism. Liberalism saw the free market as an interaction of conflicting individual interests that would eventually produce the greatest good for the greatest number of people. Liberalism did not then, and does not now, begin with an integrating vision of the whole but rather with the assumption that the individual is the starting point in economic, political, and social arrangements. Liberalism believes that the common good will result from the self-actualization of each part.

The cultural bias of this liberal world-view is clearly revealed when we look at it from the perspective of the poor in the third world. Liberation theologians in Latin America remind us frequently that those who are oppressed are oppressed as a group and can only be liberated as a people. The starting point of social consciousness is "we," not "I." When the Jewish people recall their experience of oppression at the time of Passover, they say, "*We* came out of Egypt."

Liberal economics is based on a belief in an "invisible hand" that guides the competition between the various interests in the free market—for the benefit of all. In political terms, liberalism endorses the belief that the good of all is enhanced when each group pursues its own interests. It is inherently sympathetic to pluralism and stresses the social virtue of tolerance and individual rights. Culturally, liberals tend to believe that the more individuals have the freedom to express their thoughts and feelings, the greater will be the benefit to society as a whole.

The role of government is one of management, balancing the various conflicting interests in the economy and society. Its role is to facilitate rather than to direct. "The liberal managerial style does not...directly and positively promote 'the common good.' Rather, it 'encourages' it negatively by strengthening countervailing forces and offering opportunities for progress."[17]

In one form or another, liberalism has formed the basis for the socio-economic systems of the nations of the West. The three political parties in Canada, for example, can be analyzed as variations of liberalism.[18] Walter Russell Mead holds that the American empire is, in fact, an empire shaped by liberalism. In his book, *Mortal Splendor: The American Empire in Transition,* he argues that the rise of the American empire coincides with the flourishing of liberalism from the groundwork laid from 1933 to 1952 by Franklin D. Roosevelt and Harry S. Truman. This liberal empire reached its peak, according to Mead, during the Kennedy-Johnson years. Mead describes the period after 1968 as the time of "the decline of the liberal empire."[19]

The contributions of liberalism to Western civilization are many. Its emphasis on freedom of conscience and the tolerance necessary in a pluralistic society can be fully appreciated only when we think of the various forms of authoritarianism that preceeded it. Yet, however much we may value this liberal tradition (politically, economically, or socially), we must face the fact that it has reached its limits.

This is most obviously true in the area of the economy. Liberalism works as long as the economic pie keeps expanding enough to sustain the belief that there will eventually be more for everyone.

It relies on a developing and expanding market to undergird its belief that there will be more for everybody if individual interests are allowed to interact freely on the open market. Liberalism presumes economic growth; it flounders in a time of economic scarcity, when the economic pie begins to shrink. What happens when, for whatever reason, economic growth seems less possible? The liberal ideology falters when the economic pie cannot keep expanding fast enough to maintain the illusion that there will be more for everyone in the future.

Liberalism cannot deal with the reality of limits. Once the size of the economic pie begins to shrink or just remains the same, liberals are faced with the necessity of making choices between the benefits to some at the cost to others. As the necessity of establishing social policy and priorities becomes more obvious, liberalism seems even more ill-equipped to respond to the challenge. Hence, the crisis of liberalism now making itself felt in North America and elsewhere. Bereft of any common social vision, liberals search for some basis upon which to make decisions about social priorities. Without a common social vision, there is little basis for appealing to anything beyond self-interest. Witness the constant consultation of the polls in an effort to find some basis for deciding what would result in the greatest good for the greatest number of people.

All of this leads us to consider the most serious limitation of liberalism: its intrinsic inability to respond to the very deep human need for a common meaning and vision. People cannot live by freedom and tolerance alone. There is no salvation by interaction alone. Pluralism without purpose leads only to a labyrinth of processes and procedures.

The crisis of liberalism is ultimately a crisis of meaning. Because liberalism has been so influential in shaping the contemporary Western world, it is not surprising that the West should be experiencing a crisis of meaning—of purpose and direction. Joe Holland often speaks of the crisis of the West in relation to the other great crises in the world: the crisis of the third world is economic, the crisis of the second world is political, and the crisis of the first world is cultural. "At the heart of culture is spirituality....So we might say that if the deeper crisis of industrial capitalism is cultural, we find a spiritual crisis at its core."[20]

This kind of crisis has provoked sociologist Robert Bellah to examine the *Habits of the Heart* in America. He has described "a liberal world so incoherent that it seems to be losing the significance of its own ideals."[21] Bellah's influential book is infused with a sense of concern that the separateness and individualism, which had freed Americans from the oppression of traditional social structures, has to be balanced by a new sense of commitment and community if people are not to self-destruct. "We seem to be hovering on the very brink of disaster, not only from international conflict but from the internal incoherence of our own society."[22]

A few significant words are noticeably absent from the liberal vocabulary today, words like sacrifice and commitment. David R. Gergen's description of the two presidential candidates in 1988 (who were both substantially liberal, despite their protestations to the contrary) sounds like a lament.

> Who will dare mention the great 'S' word again? Sacrifice? Don't hold your breath. The leading candidates...are so terrified of reality that they are running pell-mell in the other direction, outpromising each other in ways not to cost anyone a nickle.[23]

Liberals are inherently suspicious at this time of any attempt to impose a certain order on society. They seek to retrieve some sure space for individual freedom in the face of any threat to that freedom in the name of the common good. However, this liberal way of coping with decline ultimately perpetuates within itself another pattern of a declining empire: the disintegration of common meaning.

Liberals and conservatives are alike in that their patterns of coping with the decline of the empire mirror within themselves the patterns of that declining empire. As such, they offer no hope, no alternative for the future.

A THEOLOGICAL THREAD

Several writers cited in this chapter refer to the decline of the Roman empire to draw out some of the characteristics of America at this time. Walter Russell Mead notes some striking parallels:

> The rise and fall of the Roman republic was much on the minds of the founding fathers [of America]. Successful foreign wars...brought undreamed-of riches to the once-simple republic. Elections were openly bought and sold; corruption inserted itself into every cranny of the municipal government. Both rich and poor shook off the restraining bonds of custom, importing every luxury and dissipation—spiritual as well as sensual—from the conquered provinces. With the decline of civic virtue, the rich shook off their scruples and resorted to any means, however corrupt or ultimately however bloody, to seize and hold the offices of the state. The whole sordid process did not come to an end until a series of bloody civil wars, marked by attacks and reprisals, had laid waste the Roman world, exterminated the old Roman aristocracy, and replaced the Roman republic of laws and rights with an empire that worshiped its ruler as a god.[24]

However, "school of decline" thinkers do not usually refer to the intense theological debate that took place among Christians who were trying to come to grips with the implications of living in an empire in a state of decline. Their struggles provide us with some perspective on the challenge of thinking and acting in a situation of historical decline.

In the fourth century, Rome was the representative of a whole civilized way of life, a world power that was increasingly at ease with Christianity's sense of its universal mission. The first Christians had lived a very counter-cultural, catacomb existence within this empire. But since the time of Constantine, Christianity became the established religion of the empire. The Roman emperor was no longer the persecutor of Christianity but its patron.

Theologians of the fourth century had different estimations of the place of the Roman empire within salvation history. Some, like Eusebius, endowed the empire with a certain messianic quality. Others, such as Hippolytus, characterized it as the anti-Christ. In other words, some saw Rome as the new Jerusalem and others as a contemporary Babylon. To use more current terms, some saw it as having a "manifest destiny" and others saw it as an "evil empire." Then, as now, political and theological debates assumed that the empire was the center of the world.

The fall of Rome in 410 C.E. shattered the security of a whole way of life, a way of thinking, a world-view. Although the decline of Rome had been going on for some time, the sack of Rome in 410 by Alaric and the Goths epitomized the decline that had so long been denied. After this fall, there were Romans who criticized Christians for their ambivalent defense of the empire. This accusation provoked Augustine to begin to reflect theologically on the significance of the decline of Rome.[25]

Augustine has been criticized of late for his generally negative attitude toward women and the flesh. Yet, this warranted criticism should not detract from the fact that he stands out in the history of theology as someone who took an event in his own time as a point of departure for theological reflection.[26] For thirteen years, he pondered and wrote about what the decline of the Roman empire might mean in theological terms. What issued was his monumental study, *The City of God*. He concluded that Rome was neither the new Jerusalem nor Babylon, neither the vehicle of the messianic age nor the agent of the anti-Christ. It was simply an earthly city. Rome, he wrote, was an earthly kingdom, a relative mix of darkness and light, a political mix including elements of both Jerusalem and Babylon. Augustine's relativization of political entities was to prove the most significant influence on the Christian theology of history to this day. No nation, he said, was beyond redemption and no nation was assured of salvation. Augustine encouraged Christians to become involved in the politics of the day, but never absolutely so. For him, no earthly political movement or entity could compel absolute commitment.

Theologians of liberation today have developed a different approach to involvement in history and politics. They see politics

much more sharply: there are political systems of death to be resisted absolutely and political movements of liberation that compel Christian commitment. There is little point in setting an Au-
gustinian view of history and a liberationist view over against
each other. There is some value in recognizing that these two different approaches to politics were developed in two different historical situations: the one in a situation of historical decline and
the other in a situation of historical development.

For us in North America, it is important to ground our theological efforts and our religious response in the truth of our historical
moment. To do otherwise is to fail to situate our vocation in the
reality of our times. If we are disassociated from the real, rather
than the imagined, challenges of this hour, then our religious response will become dispirited—lacking in energy and vitality.

Augustine undertook the immense theological effort of trying
to comprehend the texture of his own times because he was also a
bishop pastorally engaged with the church community. He knew
that the fall of the empire posed a crucial question for the future
of the church: the choice between going with the pattern of disintegration or helping to direct an alternative future. A similar
choice faces us here, now.

A contemporary philosopher, Alasdair MacIntyre, has articulated the choice we face in this period of history. He draws parallels between the Roman and American empires and says that the
crucial turning point in the decline of Rome occurred when men
and women of good will ceased to identify with the status quo
and turned aside from the task of shoring up the empire. They set
themselves to "the construction of new forms of community within which the moral life could be sustained so that both morality
and civility might survive the coming ages of barbarism and darkness."[27]

MacIntyre maintains that we have reached just such a crucial
point. "What matters at this stage is the construction of local
forms of community within which civility...can be sustained
through the new dark ages which are already upon us."[28] His
rather startling conclusion provides us with a connecting thread
through the next chapters of this book:

This time, however, the barbarians are not waiting beyond the frontiers; they have already been governing us for quite some time. And it is our lack of consciousness of this that constitutes part of our predicament. We are waiting not for a Godot, but for another—doubtless very different—St. Benedict.[29]

"Without a vision the people perish."
Proverbs 29:18

"A young woman once said to an old woman,
What is life's heaviest burden?
And the old woman said,
To have nothing to carry."
A Jewish Tale

"I left because
I had no reason to stay."
*Former Member
of a Religious Congregation*

"We suffered in El Salvador
when we were trying to build a better life.
In the camps, we realize we still suffer
but in a more painful way.
We suffer for nothing.
We suffer without hope."
*Refugee in Mesa
Grande Camp, Honduras*

CHAPTER TWO

THE UNRAVELING
OF RELIGIOUS LIFE

As I was writing this book, there were many commemorations of the twenty-fifth anniversary of the death of President John F. Kennedy. In the United States and throughout the empire, there were scores of articles and programs to mark this tragic event. In conversations about that fateful moment in Dallas, I discovered that there were many people who, like myself, remembered exactly what they were doing and where they were when they heard the news of Kennedy's assassination.

Why do so many people, even now, consider this president's death as very significant? Some of the feelings associated with Kennedy had to do, no doubt, with the man himself. Yet, one senses that, in a way, he seems larger than life. He is a symbol of everything promising in liberal America at the height of its political and economic power. He embodied a vision and dared to ask others to sacrifice themselves for the sake of this vision. His famous words "Ask not what your country can do for you but what you can do for your country" sounded a challenge that few politicians today would dare to issue.

When Kennedy was assassinated it was as if the vision revealed itself as mortal. With the Vietnam war, the empire overstretched its limits and the intrinsic limitations of liberalism began to make themselves felt. A demoralized nation would eventually turn to the great master of illusion Ronald Reagan in the hope of reclaiming some sense of that lost vision.

For Catholics in the United States, John Kennedy also symbolized their confident entrance into mainstream America. They were ready to leave behind the "ghetto Catholicism" that had nourished the faith of the immigrant church. A similar confidence was animating the church in English-speaking Canada. In Quebec, a quiet revolution was underway in which Catholics would throw off their dependence on the institutional church as the protector of their nationalist aspirations.[1] Vatican II coincided with the kind of secular optimism animating the church in various regions on this continent. Even if Vatican II had not happened, Catholics in North America were ready and willing to enter "the modern world."

DISCOVERING AMERICA

Catholics began to discover America anew just when the liberal empire had reached its peak. Yet, as sociologist John Coleman has pointed out, their confidence was not matched by any critical sense of the culture. The United States had been, in general, rather good to the Catholic immigrants who arrived on its shores. It offered them economic opportunities not available to them in the older worlds they had left behind. As a result, the American bishops tended to be rather uncritical of the American way. "Catholic leadership has always been relatively benign and, at times, inordinately enthusiastic toward the American political, social and economic ethos."[2] If there was any criticism, it was restricted to issues such as sexuality, censorship, or those involving distributive justice for Catholics.

COPING WITH AMERICA:
LIBERALS AND CONSERVATIVES

The death of Kennedy and the Vietnam war were the clearest signals that the social fabric of America was starting to come apart at the seams. Many Americans, including many Catholics, began to feel as if their personal lives were unraveling. The seams of the social fabric no longer held and the tightly woven religious culture of American Catholicism was also beginning to loosen. For liberal Catholics, this loosening promised a liberation from the strictures of the traditional church. They welcomed this loosening and the spaces it opened within ecclesiastical structures from which to fashion a church more relevant to the times.

There was tremendous energy and even excitement around the possibility of modernizing the church. There was an explosion of theological reflection, bold experiments with the liturgy, and various attempts to restructure the parish and other organizations within the church. However, it is now becoming more apparent that rethinking and reorganizing cannot, in themselves, reweave the deep fabric of the Catholic culture. The Catholic church community has, in the past, been formed by a sacramental principle, by shared stories and symbols of meaning. John Coleman has used the word "resymbolization" to describe the challenge facing post-Vatican II American Catholicism.

> A people prospers only when it lives out of richly textured communal symbols and achieves its own unique sense of history, heroes and collective story....Today, however, Catholic America, like the larger nation, is a land without adequate symbols.[3]

Catholic conservatives have identified (almost viscerally) the lack of "adequate symbols" and meaning in the liberal, post-Vatican II church. They lament the loss of the beauty of the traditional liturgy and the demise of the ordered way of life that had characterized Catholicism. They harbor the hope of returning to previous interpretations of the central symbols of the faith, to former practices and clear statements of the teaching of the church.

Since the time of Vatican II, the church in North America has been marked by the conflict between its liberals and conservatives. This was the conflict that characterized most of the stories covered at *Catholic New Times*, a conflict that has become, as I said earlier, all too predictable.

There are those who have interpreted this conflict as a strictly intra-ecclesial struggle between the liberals and the conservatives (either closer to home or farther away in the Vatican). It is true that this conflict has a particular ecclesial genesis and history. Indeed, one could say that the ruling conservative powers in the church, only barely dislodged by the liberals at Vatican II, have once again reasserted their efforts to control the church.

Yet, this obvious internal struggle often blinds Catholics, both liberals and conservatives, to the ways in which their positions mirror the patterns of coping in a culture that has lost a sense of common vision and meaning. Many Catholics remain largely unconscious of the extent to which the church, which has become so tied to the culture of the first world, shares in the sense of social dislocation in the West. Interestingly enough, journalists seem to have a sixth sense about the social significance of the conflicts in the church. Writers who never spilled much ink over church matters are now willing to devote considerable time and space to covering the latest dispute between a liberal theologian and the Vatican. It is as if they recognize that the conflict being played out within the church is also being played out in the wider culture.

Catholic conservatives rail against the disintegration of values in the culture and feel the absence of any unifying vision in the church which would provide them with some defense against the corrosive effects of the chaos in the culture. These conservatives are in touch with the dangers of life within a declining culture—but only selectively so. Their legitimate concerns about the perils of individual autonomy and the cultural addiction to pleasure have blinded them to the extent to which they have internalized at least one pattern of decline within the empire: the imperialistic use of power. The parallels with the general conservative tendency in this culture (mentioned in the previous chapter) seem obvious. Conservatives would like to impose order in the church through legislation, through disciplinary action, and through restricting power in the church to those members of the hierarchy who share their agenda.

However, the conservative agenda, which seeks some forms of protection against the disintegration of the culture, ends up maintaining a fatal link between the church and the declining empire. It is the dying illusion of any empire, religious or secular, to think that an integrating and ordering vision can be constructed or reconstructed through the coercive use of power.

Liberal Catholics are more aware that calls for "unity" in the church sometimes cloak an effort to justify the imposition of rigid uniformity in the church. They are quite rightly suspicious that such a "unity" (i.e., uniformity) would serve only to increase the control of certain groups within the church. In the face of the conservative effort to reassert one view of the church as the only one, liberals espouse human rights and democratic freedoms in the church. They advocate greater pluralism and tolerance for individual conscience in the areas of faith and morality.

Yet, this suspicion about the conservatives renders many liberals insensitive to the deep human desire for a common vision to live by. Catholic liberals are wary of the traditional calls to sacrifice and commitment. Although they are critical of conservative tendencies in the church, they tend to be less critical of the liberal culture. As a result, they become more vulnerable to the generalized trend toward economic selfishness, the psychologies and spiritualities of self-development. Thus, the liberal option in the church ultimately mirrors another pattern of decline within the culture.

It is tragic, but all too often true, that liberals and conservatives in the church have so mirrored each other in reverse that they have lost sight of how both groups reflect and even confirm the patterns of decline in the culture. For this reason, neither group opens up a real option for the future of the church or of the culture. My sense is that the liberal and conservative options are too tied to this culture to provide religious congregations with a way of threading their way into the future. Little wonder that religious life, which weaves and is woven on the larger framework of church and society, is beginning to unravel.

I turn now to examining the ways the disintegrating patterns in the culture have become internalized in religious life in North America. The extent of this internalization is not due to personal weakness on the part of individual members of religious congregations. In general, religious are not weak. They are often great-spirited and usually great-hearted people. No, the extent of this internalization is due to the powerful and pervasive quality of Western culture as it is embodied in the system of the American empire. To admit the negative power of this system is the first step toward naming not so much our own personal weakness but the positive power of collective resistance called for at this time.

There is little point in blaming ourselves or others for problems that are so intertwined with the structures in which we all participate. We would do well to spend less energy on blaming and more energy in assuming responsibility for where we go from here.

RELIGIOUS LIFE BEHIND THE PLASTIC CURTAIN

In this section, I shall explore the ways in which the economic system of the empire (capitalist consumerism) has affected the value system of religious life. Then I shall examine the ways in which the socio-political form of the empire (liberalism) has influenced religious life at this time.

Liberals and conservatives in North America are alike in their basic belief in the free enterprise system inaugurated by nineteenth-century industrial capitalism. This economic system has so transformed every dimension of our lives that we can now speak of a whole culture, the consumer culture, that has been shaped by the values of materialism. As the president of Czechoslovakia, Vaclav Havel, has observed, "Materialism may have failed as an ideology in the East, but it has certainly triumphed as a matter of practice in the West."[4]

The basic world-view of consumerism (and its inherent subversion of the world-view of the gospel) has been articulated with great insight and clarity by John Kavanaugh S.J. in his influential book *Following Christ in a Consumer Society*. No one can read this book and remain with the innocent sense that consumerism is merely about shopping. Kavanaugh's central point is that consumerism is a whole way of life, a coherent system of values and attitudes propagated through the most sophisticated means of advertising. I found his analysis of advertising particularly disturbing in the light of my own research on the effectiveness of the Nazi propaganda about the Jews. Propaganda, I discovered, has little to do with the truth and reality; it succeeds because anything repeated often enough becomes "true."

According to Kavanaugh, consumerism is a materialistic way of life which rests on a fundamental inversion of the values of the Judaeo-Christian tradition: in consumerism, things become more important than persons. This inversion, or perversion, of values is subtly present, for example, in the advertisements for cars (symbol of the speed and self-direction of America).

The car appears, whether on a television screen or on the magazine page, with a certain feel to it. The fender almost bends a smile and the headlights seem to see ahead. It appears almost alive, like a person; it makes you feel that you will become a real person if you buy it. The car is worth buying, worth selling yourself for, which is what the woman next to the car is doing. Wound up like a mechanical doll, with metallic hair and spikey eyelashes, she has become a thing to sell, an expensive item that promises people that they will become "someone" if they buy it.

This is a simple and familiar example of the inversion of values and fundamental relationships. Persons begin to serve things instead of things being made to serve persons. In biblical terms, this perversion is called idolatry. In contemporary terms, it results in the most subtle forms of enslavement: persons produce and produce in order to consume many things and so they are consumed as persons in the process. The cravings induced by advertising, which are so necessary to the free-market system, seduce people into a more or less permanent state of captivity. Within the culture of consumerism, the line between the necessary and the superfluous becomes blurred. The advertising of the consumer culture creates cravings within us that begin to seem almost natural. A car begins to seem less like a luxury and more like a necessity of life. The need for a car becomes "second nature" to us.

The followers of the creed of consumerism believe that they have to have "more," "bigger," "better," "the latest," or "the new and improved" in order to be someone. They believe not only that having more means being more but also that looking good means being good. But looking good and being more depend on producing more, earning more, and selling oneself on the open market. The incentive to produce more never ends because there is always "more" to consume. There is never "enough": not enough time, not enough money, not enough self.

There is little room in the world of consumerism for those who seem unproductive: the elderly, the unemployed, the handicapped, etc. Even those who are productive live with the lurking fear that they might not be as productive forever. They are anxious that they too, like so many of the commodities they have consumed, may become disposable.

The modalities of consumerism are all too easily internalized in our patterns of relating to others and to God. We grow up in this culture believing that love is something to be earned or purchased. We are culturally biased toward relating to others along the lines of the marketplace: competition, domination, and manipulation.

Most religious would not identify with the crasser forms of consumerism. Yet, it would be naive to think that we are above "buying" at least some of the values being held out to us constantly through the media. Consider the amount of time in front of the television that the average American spends absorbing the worldview of consumerism:

> Estimates of the average American watching-time run from 26 hours a week to the equivalent of 13 straight continuous years of our average life span. Since up to 27 percent of prime time can be given to advertisement, we could possibly spend, on an average, the equivalent of *three solid years* watching solely commercials[5] [emphasis mine].

Assuming that most religious watch some television, we have to consider the possibility that they are at least as much formed by the creed of consumerism as by the gospel of Jesus Christ. If religious watch as much television as the average American, their formation for becoming consumers will be *three solid years* of watching advertisements. By most standards, that is a pretty solid formation program! It is all the more effective because it is so subtle and all-pervasive. The problem is that they aren't conscious of the fact that they have entered into this formation program. They usually don't notice when they have become professed members of the consumer culture.

Ours is a peculiar form of captivity. We do not live behind an iron curtain but we do live behind a plastic curtain. The first step in liberating ourselves must begin with a consciousness of captivity in our culture. In some situations the prophetic call involves saying to those who are oppressed, "Go free." But in other situations, such as our own, the prophetic task is to say to those who think they are free, "You are in captivity." Just as the values of consumerism pervade every dimension of our societal lives, so too is it beginning to permeate every dimension of our lives as religious: our prayer, our apostolic and community life. In the reflections that follow, I shall explore how some of the contemporary problems in religious life are really symptoms of the extent to which we live in captivity behind the plastic curtain.

Supermarket Spirituality

The basic materialism of consumerism tends to corrode any authentic sense of spirituality. Spirituality is the salt in any form of religious life, but it can tend to become rather insipid in this culture. The consuming belief that love and life are to be earned and bought militates against the deepest faith of people formed by the biblical tradition: faith in God's gratuitous love for us. This is not something we could ever have earned. This free gift, this graciousness, invites us to live in the most fundamental religious attitude, a spirit of gratitude. This sense of gratefulness prompts us to worship, to pray, and to give freely of ourselves. This is the basis for any authentic Christian spirituality.

Yet, in my experience as a retreat director, I have often felt how difficult it is to evoke in a retreatant even the desire for the grace of gratitude. The more I reflect on our captivity behind the plastic curtain, the more I see that a retreatant's lack of openness to the desire for gratitude has less to say about that person's openness and more to say about how closed this culture is to the graciousness of life.

It is equally difficult, in a culture that values things more than persons, to discover a deep personal relationship with God. Without an awareness of God as a person, without a personal relationship to God, religious life makes little sense. Religious congregations can function without this central relationship to a personal God but they cannot flourish. And, at a certain point, merely functioning makes most people begin to feel dysfunctional.

A god who becomes the "object" of our attention, however prayerfully, easily becomes a god shaped by our needs and wants and projections. This god is easy to cut down to size, easy to domesticate and shape in our own (masculine or feminine) image. This god asks little of us and gives much by way of legitimizing whatever we are about. Prayer is then our way of using god for our own interests—for our personal development or as the legitimation of various projects. Our culture accepts and even approves of this kind of prayer as "healthy" or "useful."

We relate to God and to others in a correlative way: if we treat God as a thing, we lose a sense of the infinite value of each person; if we treat persons as things, we tend to reduce God to the status of some "thing," however big, in our lives. When God becomes a thing, it is easily compartmentalized and our prayer to such a god becomes predictable and dispassionate.

All of these dilemmas presume that we take time to pray. However, it is more than possible, in this culture, to begin to see time for prayer as unproductive and, therefore, useless. Being with God seems as useless an activity as being with other people often is. Wasting time is not socially acceptable.

Our culturally induced desire for "results" in prayer may take various forms: the desire for an answer, for some clarity, for a feeling of consolation, or for some experience of God. The frustration of these desires can lead to shopping around for various spiritual experiences. In this case, the desire to consume many things has been subtly transformed into the desire to accumulate experiences of whatever sort.

Shopping is a consumer skill that religious, like others in this culture, learn by making the rounds of supermarkets and malls. The enormous variety of commodities puts shoppers in a situation of "overchoice."[6] There are often so few differences among all the products that it really doesn't matter what you choose.

Religious who want to shop around for spiritual experiences need only consult the summer listings in Catholic newspapers. The ads for workshops, retreats, and courses are geared toward religious consumers. They illustrate the wide variety of religious experiences available and the "latest" in spiritual trends. One year there are many workshops on Ignatian spiritual direction. The next year, mini-courses on dreams are popular and the following year there is a run on sessions for adult children of alcoholics. I do not want to trivialize the value of these experiences—they have clearly been helpful for many people—but I do want to note that there can be fads in spirituality just as there are changing perceptions of what is fashionable in the wider culture. Directors of retreat houses and renewal centers have told me that their biggest challenge is that of planning programs that will "capitalize" on the "latest" development in spirituality. They have to look for speakers who are "hot" on the lecture circuit.

This abundance of spiritual experiences may be interpreted positively as a sign of the deep spiritual hunger in our culture. This hunger exists and, as I will suggest in Chapter Four, North Americans are tending to nourish their desire for spirituality outside of the institutional churches. Nevertheless, there is a down side to all of this. The surfeit of spiritualities tends to form a consumer who moves from religious experience to religious experience, barely digesting one before another is tasted. The "overchoice" in the area of spirituality tends to deflect from the development of spiritual depth. The temptation to discard one type of spirituality, once it fails to produce the desired "experience," is considerable. The collective wisdom of spiritual guides over the centuries suggests that this temptation should be resisted.

Shopping around for the fashionable and the fitting can lead to avoiding the spiritual stripping down that is an essential stage in the development of a mature life of faith.

Those wise in the ways of faith and love have written at length about the importance of staying with prayer precisely at the moment when it seems most useless and unproductive. The point at which God is no longer experienced is the point at which one experiences, in faith, that God is greater than one's experience of God. This is the point at which we pass over from the experience of being loved by God to the possibility of loving God, from the experience of being from God to being for God. We live in a culture of such artificial light that we can lose a sense of the value of passing through a "dark night" or a "way of purgation." In the midst of this most overdeveloped world, we run the risk of remaining spiritually underdeveloped.

"Productive" Ministries

The most socially acceptable area of religious life today is that of ministry. In a productivity-oriented culture, even non-religious people can appreciate the fact that sisters, brothers, and priests "do good work." And it is true that we do much good. Most religious work very hard in their demanding ministries of service.

However, this social approval is quickly withdrawn once religious begin to work for changes in the socio-economic system which is fueled by the activities of producing and consuming. The educational work of religious is appreciated, for example, as long as they do not begin teaching students to become more critical of liberal capitalism. The system conspires to keep us productive rather than prophetic. We are kept very busy. We are offered economic benefits and securities for making the system work and we are rewarded for competence and efficiency.

Productive but not prophetic. There is no doubt that what we religious are doing is often of immeasurable value for others. However, the busyness involved in producing good and even just works fosters the illusion in us (personally and collectively) that we are really going somewhere. It may be that we are merely running on the spot. It is in the best interests of the empire that we are kept busy, so busy that we do not have time to stop and think about where this will all end up. We do not have time to stop and question the process of doing good, which is consuming us as persons and as religious. This busyness affects those involved in more traditional apostolates as well as those engaged in newer forms of ministry. We are so busy responding to the needs in the church or in our congregations, or to the latest issues, that we do not have time to question what is being done and for whom and why. As long as we keep spinning around, we will probably not notice that the fabric of society—and of religious life—is beginning to unravel.

I must confess to having tried to cope with my own busyness through the various means suggested in this society. At one point, I even tried time management until I realized that I was just managing to get more work in. I started to notice other patterns of coping with the pressures of productivity. A relative of mine awoke one day with the realization that she was killing herself at work to get the money to take expensive vacations so she could get away and recuperate from the rat race. More and more religious crossed my path on the way to a renewal progam to recover from burnout. The programs were marvelously life-giving for these people—who usually then returned to the kind of work that had been so death-dealing in the first place. Perhaps we in religious congregations need to reflect on whether we are using renewal programs as a way of recycling burned-out people so that they can become productive again. Perhaps we should ask whether the widespread burnout among active religious should be treated as a *personal problem* affecting some people—or as a *symptom* of a larger cultural problem which is becoming internalized in religious congregations.

It would be too simplistic to say that we should stop "doing" in order to practice a little more "being." This dualistic view of life, sometimes stated as the difference between action and contemplation, obscures the reality that doing is often a way of being and "just being" often involves profound activity. It may be truer to say that the challenge facing us at this moment is to find a greater coherence between what we do and who we are. As I look back over my own work experiences, I am amazed to discover that fatigue rarely had anything to do with the number of hours worked or the difficulties involved. Fatigue crept in when I was not doing what I deeply wanted to do, when (as Karl Marx would say) I was alienated from my own work. When there was a sense of coherence between my life and my work, I could work very hard but not be consumed in the process. I began to feel fatigued when I started to doubt why I was doing what I was doing, when the meaning of my activity was no longer clear. In retrospect, I had more than enough energy and enthusiasm when my work had coherence and meaning. The structures of this society and, indeed, of the church, often alienate religious from their own work, leaving them with a sense that what they are doing does not really reflect who they are. The point is that simply being productive alienates us from the prophetic dimension of our lives.

When productivity becomes an end in itself, the loss of a sense of greater purpose begins to make itself felt in either laziness or further busyness. For some, a lack of purpose deprives them of a desire to work. For others, the sense of purposelessness is manifested in indiscriminate involvement in whatever is at hand. This may partly explain some of the tensions in community between those who see each other as underworked or overworked. Busy people become exceedingly frustrated with those they perceive as "not pulling their weight." Lazy people are often willing to analyze the "workaholism" of those more active. In the process, both groups, positively or negatively, are reinforcing the consuming pattern of productivity in religious life.

It may be instructive to recall that, in general, neither busyness nor laziness were the usual problems of the more traditional form of religious life. Although work had a definite place in the order of the day, it was never allowed to take over the whole of one's life. The daily structure of community life ensured that there was time for leisure, or "recreation" as it was called. This was the time to do nothing but be together. There was also time set aside to do nothing but be with God in prayer. Within such a structure, work became neither absolute nor irrelevant. Apostolic life was related to a larger framework of meaning. To the extent that a person freely chose this structure of life, one's work was not alienated from one's being. Now, however, it seems clearer that, for many, this structure seemed more imposed from without, rather than a means freely chosen by those within it. The pressure of productivity is one of the ways in which the power of the empire prevents religious from working to seriously undermine the status quo. A second way is through the subtle seduction of economic benefits and job security. In a time of rising unemployment and of economic insecurity within congregations, religious are understandably vulnerable to these considerations. Higher salaries, medical and dental benefits, retirement packages and job security (through tenure, etc.) are hardly realities that religious can afford to take lightly these days. Yet, these same benefits and securities rely on the continuance of established institutions or organizations and on the persistence of the present economic order. All of which serves to mute any radical objections that religious might have about the status quo in North America. These are some of the threads that tie us to the present fabric of society.

Religious (and lay people) who work within church structures often face an entirely different set of problems; there is little job security, few economic benefits, and rarely such a thing as a "just" wage. Religious women, who for generations provided the church with "cheap labor," are not willing to tolerate this situation any longer. Nor are lay people who want to become involved in the ministry of the church on more than a volunteer basis. Having participated in several efforts to negotiate a work contract with priests and bishops, I am convinced that the question of job security is as important for developing new structures in the church as the question of a just salary. As long as lay people and religious can be fired at whim by the clergy, the clerical control of the church will remain fundamentally intact, no matter now many non-clerical people are working within it.

Yet, there is an ambiguity in our efforts to create a more just working situation within the church. It is precisely these hard-won securities and benefits that could, in the long run, jeopardize any effort toward basic social change within the church itself.

Benefits and securities depend on a contract which clearly identi-
fies the employer. At this point in history, this kind of contract
tends to reinforce the control of the clergy even as the contract
attempts to restrain it. The ambiguity for religious, in the church
as in society, is that the more we receive benefits and security
from a system, the less likely we are to change that system radically.

The third way the empire co-opts our work is through the social approval given to competence and efficiency. I do not want to
romanticize incompetence or to spiritualize it in any way. Many
older female religious can recall the days when the urgent needs
of education and lack of money made it necessary for them to
"teach on their crucifix," i.e., without the appropriate and necessary training. The movement to educate religious, which began in
the 1950s (e.g., The Sister Formation Program) has borne enormous fruit. Education and a deeper personal formation gave
many religious the confidence to transform traditional apostolates
or to initiate new forms of service.

Nevertheless, we were perhaps unaware of how, in being educated and trained, we were also assimilating a cultural sense of
the value of professional competence and efficiency. Within this
culture, competence and efficiency are sometimes more ends in
themselves than means to some end.

In my experience, one's sense of competence can get in the way
of responding to the call of the poor, to those who cannot make it
in a world defined by productivity. I became aware of my own
cultural deformation while working at *Catholic New Times* in its
first fragile years. We had founded this newspaper explicity to
provide a voice for those who had no voice—in the church and in
our country. Those who watched this little newspaper grow considered it exciting and courageous. Sometimes it seemed that
way, but most of the time the work was drudgery. And frustrat-
ing. The precarious nature of our finances made it impossible to
buy the necessary equipment, to rent space to work in, or to hire
enough staff so that we did not have to do the work of several
people. We lived in fear of postal rate increases. The lack of money meant lack of time, energy, and equipment. As a result, more

was left undone than done, the newspaper was full of typos and it looked tacky. What we wrote late at night did not always stand up in the clear light of day. It was humiliating.

I vented my frustrations with Mary Power R.S.C.J., who was working as a volunteer at the time. I ranted on about how difficult it was to share one typewriter with four other people, about the aggravating delays because there was only one phone line to use. She listened and then said wisely, "Only the rich can afford to be efficient." I learned something that day that has stood me in good stead. I made my peace with the poverty of poverty—with the inefficiency, the incompetence, and the seeming unproductiveness of it all. It takes money to have the time and equipment to work quickly. It takes money to have all the qualified people necessary to make things work well. No matter how competent and efficient individuals may be, an organization's lack of money will render them all slightly incompetent and inefficient. It is the rare group involved in social change that can afford to work *as* the rich *for* the poor.

And even if they could, should they? Most religious involved in justice work must come to some peaceful choice about working *as* the poor if they are going to work with and for the poor. If religious have thoroughly assimilated the cultural value of efficiency as an end in itself, then they are less likely to undertake the kind of work that is limited by the constraints of poverty. The cultural norm of efficiency may make us less, not more, able to undertake work directed toward serious social change.

In sum, the empire keeps us captive within itself by keeping us busy, by offering us securities and benefits, and by making a virtue of competence and efficiency. Our liberation begins when we begin to see the extent to which our finest efforts at ministry, in style if not in substance, communicates the creed of consumerism as much as the gospel of Jesus Christ.

The Consumption of Community

Community is that aspect of religious life that is the least compatible with the values of the American empire. Prayer may be valued by those who see it as an aid to psychological growth, and our ministry is appreciated by others who recognize the good we do. However, there is little cultural support for living in community. Robert Bellah has pointed out that, although there is a great hunger for community in America and a great deal of social rhetoric about the value of community, the whole socio-economic system is fundamentally shaped by the norm of individualism.[7]

To the extent that religious congregations are tied to this socio-economic system, they will experience the unraveling of community life. There are many and various efforts to cope with this unraveling: the increasing use of facilitators to help communities develop the skills of small group living, the number of workshops on interpersonal dynamics, the frequent shuffling of personnel in the hope of forming more compatible living groups, people choosing to live alone simply because they are weary of the tensions of community, the number of articles and studies on the factors that help or hinder community life.

The problems in community life are real. Unfortunately, many religious tend to see them as either personal problems or as problems internal to a congregation. This may be partly true in some situations. However, this tendency to situate a problem in a congregation makes it appear as if the solution will be found there through the efforts of individuals or a congregation as a whole. Coping with community as an internal problem may involve a further liberalization of community life or a return to some of the more traditional forms of community.

In its finest moments, the more traditional form of community life arose from a *shared meaning,* or mission. Members were gathered around a set of common symbols and were committed within mutually recognized structures and practices. Yet, at its worst moments, the cohesiveness of this way of life often resulted in a stifling conformity that inhibited personal growth and the development of creative responses to the needs of the times. The liberalization of religious life at the time of Vatican II loosened the threads of this former fabric of religious life.

In the first phase of this loosening, religious attempted to live more closely together in small communities. There was a desire for more *sharing and meaningful relationships.* Some soon found that these smaller groups could be as stifling as the more traditional communities and sometimes even more conflict-ridden. There was a tendency for some groups to move, consciously or not, into the mode of a therapeutic community.

In the second phase, there has been movement to structure communities more in terms of the needs of ministry. Community is defined in terms of *meaningful ministry*. For some, community became primarily a base for personal ministry, and the structures of community were adjusted to facilitate the wide diversity of individual commitments to ministry. The diversification of ministries coincided with the development of diversified forms of community life: intercongregational groups, clustering, support groups, etc. Most religious congregations now face the challenge of trying to find the basis for unity in the midst of a plurality of work and lifestyles.

And what will be the next phase of religious life? The answer, I suspect, lies in the formulation of a *common meaning* that moves through and beyond the personal relationships or ministries of community members. Our search may be for a community constituted first as an act of faith and hope.

The Vatican's Congregation on Religious and Secular Institutes (CRIS, later changed to Congregation of Institutes for Consecrated Living [CICL]) and some conservative groups, reacting to the pluralism engendered by the liberalization of religious community, have attempted to impose a certain order on what they see as the rather disorderly way of life characteristic of American religious. Through issuing the 1983 curial document, *The Essential Elements in the Church's Teaching on Religious Life,* and through the pressure exerted as religious congregations brought forth their new constitutions for Vatican approval, conservatives attempted to reverse the liberal trend. The message was clear: return to some of the more traditional structures of religious life. The lack of respect for the integrity of religious congregations was so obvious that anyone with a liberal bone in the body justifiably reacted to this blatant abuse of authority. The Roman attempt to impose order on congregations has made some religious wonder whether they have become too tied into the fabric of the official church.

As I mentioned in the Introduction, the arrogant Vatican critique of the more liberal form of religious life has made it difficult for us to seriously examine problems in community life today. We tended to see community as an internal problem; now Rome is forcing us to treat it as an internal conflict in the church, which needs to be solved in the church. Given this restricted sense of the problem, a solution becomes even more difficult to imagine.

The problem of community life seems deeper, and even different, as we become more critical of the culture we live in. The very core of community, the commitment to the gospel, is being consumed. Behind the plastic curtain, where productivity is paramount, time spent merely being in community can appear as wasted time. We are tempted to cut down on the amount of time together and call for more "quality time." Even when we spend time together, it is difficult to relate precisely as persons. We are likely to feel more comfortable thinking of each other as co-workers and relating to each other through contractual agreements to produce something or to do something together. It is more difficult for us who live in a plastic culture to resist the temptation to treat others as disposable when their usefulness is over. In a plastic culture, it is harder to value more permanent relationships and commitments. Given the all-pervasive dynamic of the marketplace, we are more tempted to abandon the struggle to live and work co-operatively. Most significantly, in a materialistic culture, it has become more difficult for us to sustain a vital sense of the spiritual purpose and meaning of being together. Is it any wonder that community is a problem? Perhaps it is more appropriate to say that it is a symptom of the profound problem of the socio-economic system we live in.

RELIGIOUS LIFE IN THE LIBERAL EMPIRE

In the previous section, I explored ways in which religious have internalized some of the characteristics of late industrial capitalism. Now I will examine the patterns in the political system that are correlative to the socio-economic system of capitalism. My sense is that many of the problems of religious life in North America reflect the crisis of liberalism in the West. I do not want to imply that all congregations in North America are liberal. Some are definitely more conservative or traditional and there are conservative elements in every congregation. However, the dominant mode in most religious congregations is the liberal.

Liberal religious have brought many gifts to the church. Often these gifts are not recognized or welcomed because they call for a new response on the part of the church. The calls that liberals issue (for more freedom and tolerance in the church, for a greater pluralism and openness) are those that the hierarchical church ignores at its own peril. It has tended to resist any changes in its closed and uniform system. Thus, its officials always seem to be criticizing liberalism from without rather than from within.

The weightiest criticism of the liberal model of religious life will come from those who have lived its potential. Members of more liberal religious congregations are much more able to examine liberalism from within their own experience: from their appreciation of its strengths and from their compassion for its weaknesses. However, if we look only at the criticisms emanating from the institutional church, we probably spend most of our energy extolling the virtues of the liberal model of religious life. If, on the other hand, we take a hard look at our culture, we will be more inclined to take a closer look at the limitations of the liberal model. It depends on our angle of vision. My experience is that most liberals are, understandably, far more critical of the church than of the culture we live in. Nevertheless, we need to know the limits of the thread of liberalism that has become part of the fabric of our lives. We need to understand how our congregations are unraveling, even as liberalism is becoming frayed at the edges.

The Illusion of Unlimited Possibilities
In the previous chapter, I suggested that liberalism relies on a situation of expanding economic possibilities in order to sustain the belief that there will be more for everyone in the future if individual interests are allowed to develop fully. This economically based belief in unlimited possibilities can become transformed into the

social belief that each person can and should develop themselves fully.

Liberalism begins to flounder, however, when the economic potential begins to diminish. The illusion of unlimited possibilities can be maintained but the facts cannot be denied forever. The majority of the people in the world have long faced the facts: there are limits to economic and personal growth. In very few countries have people internalized the belief that they have unlimited possibilities that can and should be developed. Few nations are based on the belief of the unlimited right to the "pursuit of happiness."

There are signs, however, that a significant number of religious have internalized this cultural belief in unlimited personal development and the pursuit of happiness. A considerable amount of time, energy, and money has been invested in such personal growth. Liberal congregations invest a great deal in this in the hope that the greater personal development of each individual will ultimately result in the greater good of all. Some of this is a welcome evolution, especially given the relative neglect of personal development in the more traditional form of religious life. However, this pursuit of personal development can become extreme. This has been the subject of some humorous conversations in communities. The following is the text of a flyer that has found its way to several congregations in the United States and Canada:

> OBITUARY 1950: Sr. Immaculata, aged 86, died in the infirmary of the motherhouse today while the Sisters chanted the traditional "Salve Regina" around her bed. Sister Immaculata had taught for 62 years in the elementary schools of her Order before retiring to the infirmary. Sister's 62 years touched the hearts of thousands of children.

> OBITUARY 1999: Sister Becky Thompson, aged 86, died during a sensitivity session of the Community Center while the other three members of her Order looked on in surprise. Sister Thompson had been a school teacher for 1 year, a spiritual director for 1 year, a youth minister for 1 year, a liturgist

for 1 year, a nurse for 1 year. The other 57 years of Sister Thompson's religious life were spent in various schools preparing to become a teacher, a spiritual director, a youth minister, and a nurse. Sister's five years of active religious life were an inspiration to all.

As humorous as these obituaries are, they raise the troublesome question of what happens to the soul of religious life when the pursuit of personal happiness becomes the focus of an individual or a congregation. What happens when this liberal illusion crashes on the shoals of the reality of limits? What happens to a liberal congregation when it faces the reality of scarcity—diminishing numbers, diminishing financial resources? Who would set limits to this kind of personal growth, and why? Leadership groups often find themselves struggling to answer questions like these. They are left with the impossible task of trying to balance the various conflicting interests and needs of the individual members.

The burden of the illusion of unlimited possibilities afflicts many apostolic congregations as they attempt to set priorities in ministry. Given the diminishment of resources, making choices seems both necessary and almost impossible. Rather than face the difficulty of making these choices, some congregations keep expanding the possibilities for individual ministry. Liberal groups, whether religious or political, lack the common vision that would compel sacrificing possibilities for personal development or commitments. Although every congregation has a stated mission, or vision, of its charism, more often than not it plays no real role as a basis for decision making. To get some sense of this, we need only ask how many religious would readily and quickly change jobs, a program of studies, lifestyle, or forego a sabbatical because it was obviously for the sake of the charism stated in the constitution?

With diminishing numbers and diminishing resources, the actualization of personal or apostolic possibilities relies more on the power and persuasion of those who desire these possibilities and on the good will and sympathy of those in decision-making roles. This situation is open to the misuse and even abuse of authority on the part of the members or those in leadership. Liberal congregations are often concerned with issues of authority and government because there is usually no authorizing vision to which both members and leadership can refer as a basis for making decisions.

Pluralism Without Purpose

For many congregations in the 1970s the diversity of lifestyles and ministries was seen as an important step beyond the uniformity of the more traditional model. Pluralism was thought to be the means for responding to new and urgent calls in the modern world. Twenty years later, there is reason to ask whether pluralism in religious life has become an end in itself. Lost in this increasing pluralism is a sense of the purpose of it all. In some congregations, there has been such a diffusion of energies that it is difficult to see what remains in common. Members have some vague sense of belonging to a group which is usually sustained by a vague ethos or spirit, by memories of a shared history, by a shared sense of responsibility for elderly members, and by relationships with those who are co-workers, friends, or like-minded allies.

But belonging is not the same as commitment.[8] Commitment in a congregation is sustained by a meaningful vision that is more than the sum of the personal dreams and interests of the individual members. Liberals may be very committed to their work, to some issue, or to some people, while being content to simply "belong" to their congregation.

We are very tolerant of the wide diversity of lifestyles and ministries in our congregations. This tolerance has become one of the primary virtues in liberal congregations. We call it "openness" or "respect" or "trusting one another" or "empowering each other." Our tolerance seems limitless. Has it become a terminal tolerance? Michael Crosby O.F.M. Cap. has described the debilitating reality of liberal tolerance in a local community. "We can accept almost anything now...because we've had to accept everything."[9] Yet, Crosby also makes the perceptive comment that there is a limit to this liberal tolerance. It is intolerant of anything that seems more radical or demanding. Anyone who wants to pray more, to act more radically, or to strengthen the commitment to community is branded as fanatical or as imposing her views on the community.

The downside of liberal tolerance is, to use the words of Crosby again, a kind of "moral minimalism." Liberal communities are held together by an agreement, stated or unstated, to do the minimum. After all the individual interests and commitments of members are taken into account, what is held in common is very minimal indeed. This process does not happen overnight, so there is usually enough time to adjust to this moral minimalism. Soon the minimum seems the normal requirement of belonging to a religious group. We become content with a few meetings, fewer times for prayer, and an occasional party to sustain our sense of belonging. The emerging problem in religious congregations is not that people are "dropping out" but that they are merely "dropping in."

Someone who left her congregation explained her reason. "I left," she said, "because I had no reason to stay." This is one of the starkest statements of the crisis of meaning in liberal religious life that I have heard.

Michael Crosby describes the sitution of religious congregations today in terms of "bureaucratic individualism," i.e., bureaucracies that use the rhetoric of community but are operationally geared toward the needs and desires of individuals. Two important roles in this kind of liberal bureaucracy are the managers who try to balance all the individual interests, and the therapists who help people cope with the effects of bureaucracy.[10] The managerial role is often performed by those on councils and the therapeutic role by those involved in formation.

Not surprisingly, it is increasingly difficult to find persons who are willing to undertake leadership positions in liberal congregations. The service of leadership, by definition, involves a care for the whole. Those who undertake this position in a liberal congregation are faced with the almost impossible task of trying to balance the wide variety of interests and concerns within the group.

Those elected for such roles are frequently those who exemplify the liberal virtues of tolerance, respect for the person, and openness to new possibilities. They need the skills of balancing and reconciling the various interests in a congregation and facilitating their interaction. If substantial conflicts arise, as they inevitably do, they can no more be resolved by those in leadership than by all the members together. It is no longer clear what the grounds for a resolution of substantial conflicts would be. Liberals tend to handle conflict through negotiation and compromise or simply by legitimating the various sides of a conflict through expanding the range of options that are possible within a given congregation. This diffusion of conflicts may create a temporary sense of harmony but it also tends to diffuse a common sense of meaning even further. Moral minimalism ensues—not only on the local level but also on the provincial and congregational levels.

When liberal leaders (managers or therapists) are in short supply, a congregation may sometimes decide to elect leadership groups that are inherently "balanced," i.e., representative of the various interest groups within a congregation. We can baptize this by saying we are electing people with "a diversity of gifts." It might be more honest to say that it is also a way of ensuring that no direction will be taken and few real decisions made. This fear of taking any direction that would involve excluding any possibility (of ministry or lifestyle) or of not including every group or everyone is indicative of the fundamental dilemma liberalism faces today. Many liberal congregations experience the confusion of feeling very active and very paralyzed at the same time.

I remember a conversation with Sr. Kieran Flynn, to whom this book is dedicated. She had been a provincial for the Sisters of Mercy in Rhode Island in the years after Vatican II. "That must have been difficult," I remarked. "Oh no," she replied, "it was an exciting time. It was a struggle but we knew where we wanted to go. We were trying to change the old model of religious life. It's much more difficult for provincials now. We are treading water. We don't want to go back but we don't know where ahead is."

A Summary of Patterns
Here are the patterns, or characteristics, of many liberal congregations in North America that I have observed as a resource person. These congregations face the ambiguities (and therefore the conflicts and stress) of trying to operate in a time of decline (declining

numbers, resources, etc.) in the absence of a vital and common sense of meaning and direction.

1. Statements of mission or charism that are vague and general enough to include all the various interests in a congregation.

2. Difficulty in making choices, particularly in the area of long-term planning, because there is no deeply shared vision on which to base these choices.

3. An emphasis on the personal growth and development of the members, as well as a tendency to interpret community in terms of the needs of the members, work as an individual project, and spirituality as a private concern.

4. The near impossibility of sustaining corporate commitments.

5. An increasing difficulty in finding persons for leadership positions since the service of leadership, by definition, involves caring for the whole.

6. An emphasis on the liberal virtues of leadership: tolerance, respect for the person, openness to new possibilities. The need for the leadership skill of balancing and reconciling (managing) the various interests in a congregation.

7. If liberal leaders cannot easily be found, a congregation may sometimes elect inherently "balanced" leadership groups, i.e., representative of the various interest groups within the congregation. This ensures that no direction will be taken and few choices will be made.

8. A strong belief that most problems can be solved by improving group dynamics and communications. Salvation by interaction.

9. Resolving conflicts through negotiation and compromise. Because there is no authoritative vision within which to resolve substantial conflicts, liberals tend to negotiate and compromise or to legitimize all sides of the conflict by expanding the range of options within a given congregation. This diffusion of conflicts may create a temporary sense of harmony but also tends to diffuse the sense of common meaning even further.

10. Difficulty in establishing a formation program that engenders the support of all the members. Because there is usually such a diversity of models of religious life within liberal congregations, there is no one model of formation that will satisfy the various visions of the future.

11. Instead of facing the dangers and ambiguities fostered in this liberal model, there is a tendency to deny the problems of a congregation, to blame them on certain persons or groups, to escape into work or relationships outside the congregation, to become indifferent or resigned to the problems.

12. A concern with the uses and abuses of authority (models of government, etc.) because there is no common authorizing vision to which all the members can refer.

13. A tendency to be more critical of the conservative church than of the culture in which the congregation is situated.

14. Basing corporate identity on a shared past or on personal relationships in the present. In many liberal congregations, it is the shared future that is in question.

BEYOND REPAIR?

Most of this chapter has explored how religious life is becoming more unraveled the more it is patterned along the lines of the declining American empire, which is characterized by economic consumerism and political liberalism. This has involved looking at religious life from a perspective close to the heart of the empire. From that perspective, the problems besetting religious life appear very serious indeed.

Now I turn briefly to the thoughts of a theologian who has reflected on the liberal model of religious life from his perspective at the edge of the empire. That perspective can deepen our sense of the problem even further.

Not long ago, I met Jesuit Jon Sobrino on a trip to El Salvador. I knew he had been well-educated in the first world because of my acquaintance with an American who had been a graduate student with him. "Karl Rahner said that Sobrino was the best student he ever had," my friend told me. " He would have had a brilliant future in Europe. No one could figure out why Sobrino would want to go back to a place like El Salvador." But then, the American had never been to El Salvador.

Jon Sobrino exudes keenness of mind and courage of spirit. He lives and works on the edge in a colony thoroughly dominated by the empire. His experience has brought him face to face with the idols of death. "Here we don't just believe in idols—we see them," he says.[11] He can see through the ideology of the empire and how it has become death-dealing for religious life.

Sobrino has written a critique of the personalist spiritualities that developed as an inevitable reaction against the ascetical spirituality of the traditional model of religious life. "According to the personalist theory, the vows are an apt means of bringing the religious to fulfillment as a person."[12] He holds that "this conception, though correct in what it rejects, stops at a liberal kind of Christianity and religious life."[13] According to Sobrino, personalist or liberal theologies of religious life tend to make it more "normal."

Yet, he points out, religious life is inherently not normal through the structure given to it by the vows. It is normal to marry, to be free to dispose of oneself and one's possessions. It is not normal to live a life of poverty, chastity, and obedience. The deepest crisis of religious life, according to Sobrino, arises when religious who have taken vows (which are not normal) attempt to live a normal lifestyle and do normal work. "If religious life by its very structure involves a certain abnormality, then that life will experience crisis when it seeks to become normal and when it is no longer lived in the desert or on the frontier."[14]

Sobrino would not deny the normally good work done by liberal religious but he does indicate the intrinsic contradiction involved in such a way of life.

If the apostolate and lifestyle have even a spark of madness about them, the vows will be an expression of the Christian folly of the cross. If, however, the apostolate and lifestyle are characterized by tidiness, adaptation, and acceptance of the comfortable center, then the vows will not represent a sharing in the Christian folly of the cross but will be seen, at least by the more perceptive, as responsible for a deep division in the Christian and psychological consciousness of religious.[15]

Sobrino's reflections suggest the deep division that begins to take place in religious as they attempt to adapt to life in the empire. His writings invite us to consider whether the liberal model of religious life, which opened up the more traditional model, may also be closing off the option for a more radical form of religious life.

If Sobrino is right, then the difficulties in religious life today will not easily be repaired. It will not be enough merely to put a patch on things.

The question is whether religious communities have the faith and energy to do anything more than try to patch things over. The unraveling of religious life in North America is accelerated by the fact that there has also been an internal unraveling that has everything to do with the length of the thread of their own history. Many apostolic congregations founded in the nineteenth century are finding that the fabric of their life is wearing a little thin.

There is now a well-articulated theory about "the life cycle of a religious community." It describes the high energy of the founding years, the period of expansion (usually lasting about 100 years), and the time of stabilization followed by a period of breakdown.[16] The social and ecclesiastical context of religious life in North America may have cut short the period of stabilization and hastened the period of breakdown. In any case, regardless of particular variations in this life cycle, it seems that the founding vision of a community grows dimmer with time; the thread that ties future hopes to past energies becomes weaker. "The founding experience and myth, which had been internalized by the community's early generation, is no longer felt by the members."[17] Although the founding experience and myth may be articulated in constitutions and other congregational documents, these papers in themselves do not generate the energy and commitment that characterized the years of expansion. Doubt and demoralization enter into every level of the congregation during this period of breakdown—and that doubt extends even to the purpose of the congregation:

> As the community loses its sense of identity and purpose, service to the church becomes haphazard and lacks direction. Moral norms in the community are relaxed....There is a net loss of membership through increased withdrawal and decreased recruitment of new members. [18]

In North America, the period of breakdown in many apostolic communities coincided with the period of chaos following Vatican II. Gerald Arbuckle S.M. has contributed greatly, in his important book *Out of Chaos,* to understanding this period. He compares Vatican II to a culture shock; it marked the end of the system and symbols that had given meaning to the lives of religious. After an initial period of euphoria, most congregations entered into a period of disorientation. This was only temporarily relieved by attempts to re-orient religious life through structural changes and the writing of new constitutions.

> We continued to write on mission, on the need for apostolic creativity and for communal and individual prayer, but as long as we lacked the interior conversion and right leadership, the legislation and the magnificent renewal rhetoric alone did not effect the desired revitalization.[19]

As the various attempts at external renewal faltered, congregation members began to feel fearful, angry, or even despairing. They lost a sense of identity, of a common future and meaning. This is the chaos, Arbuckle says, that is characteristic of most religious congregations at this time. "This stage of chaos is marked by confusion, a sense of drifting without purpose."[20] One of the surest signs of this chaos, in his view, is the very denial of that chaos or the debunking of any attempt to articulate or come to grips with the chaos.

The chaos of religious life within the church coincides with the chaos of liberalism in the American empire. Many feel as if we are treading water. We don't want to go back to a more traditional model of religious life or the church, but we don't know where ahead is either. It would be an illusion for us to think that we can keep treading water forever. Soon we will either go with the flow of the cultural current or we will get tired and start to sink.

Nevertheless, there is still reason to hope, if only because there are those who are still able to recognize where "back" is and who still desire to go "ahead." In conversations with individuals and groups of religious, I sensed a yearning to move beyond the present realities of religious life. This often unarticulated yearning, sometimes born out of a profound sense of pain, reveals the undeniable promise of religious life that remains in the hearts of many. Even half-formed questions reveal the presence of a Response already planted deep within and among us.

"How can we sing the song of the Lord
in a strange land?"
Psalm 137:4

"But there are times—perhaps this is one of them—
when we have to take ourselves more seriously or die;
when we have to pull back from the incantations,
rhythms we've moved to thoughtlessly,
and disenthrall ourselves, bestow
ourselves to silence, or a severer listening, cleansed
of oratory, formulas, choruses, laments, static
crowding the wires."
Adrienne Rich

"Live the questions now.
Perhaps you will then gradually,
without noticing it,
live along some distant day
into the answer."
Rainer Maria Rilke

"I said to my soul, be still,
and wait without hope
for hope would be hope for the wrong thing...."
T.S. Eliot

CHAPTER THREE

THIS THREADBARE MOMENT

This is a threadbare moment in religious life in North America. We are living through one of those in-between moments in history when the past lies in shreds and the future remains unformed. This is not a better or worse moment in religious life. It is, quite simply, the moment we are called to see through. It is a moment with its own graces and its own temptations. It is a moment to be received and to be resisted.

In the previous chapters, I have attempted to describe the unraveling of religious life in North America in terms that are largely political, social, economic, and even psychological. Yet, although these reflections may be revealing, they are not necessarily redemptive. We need to name this moment we live in with religious language in order to engage the deepest level of ourselves. Such language does not fall from heaven, nor can it be simply manufactured out of the stuff of the present. It is a language that has emerged in the space in-between the action of the Spirit and human persons. It has grown and changed in the long history of the Judaeo-Christian experience.

Given what we are up against, the most helpful language from this tradition is not the denotative language of doctrine but rather the connotative symbols and images that have the power to evoke and provoke our response to this moment in history. Symbols and images help us to name what we barely know or are too afraid to know. Never limited to any one historical understanding, symbols and images contain a "surcharge of meaning" that liberates new ways of acting and seeing.[1]

Not every symbol or image or story from the Christian tradition evokes a liberating power at this moment in history. There may be some which, although pertinent in the past or promising at some future moment, are not so now. It takes sifting and sorting to recover those symbols and images that can engage us as religious persons in this time and place. Such a process necessarily involves discernment. One of the principles for recognizing the appropriateness of symbols and images is, it seems, whether they connect us with the present reality of North America—in ways that are both critical and creative.

THE DARK NIGHT

In the course of my own sifting and sorting, I have come to appreciate the traditional image of "the dark night" as one that can connect us to the reality of this threadbare moment in our culture and our religious life.

In the writings of the great Carmelites, Teresa of Avila and John of the Cross, the image of the dark night is used to describe an important transition phase in the life of faith. The dark night is the time during which the images, feelings, and consolation of a more active form of meditation seem to disappear. It is a time when one is tempted to seek consolation wherever it can be found. Yet, it is also a time when a person is invited to be with God even without the images and the felt sense of God. In this dark night, the deeper faith and love that characterize contemplation are born. We are invited to move from the experience of being loved by God to simply loving God for no other reason than that God is God.

The grace of this dark time is the profound realization that the mysterious thread of one's life is being spun by the Spirit on a loom much larger than the one bounded by our limited human efforts. It is a time not so much of weaving but of being woven, of being knit together in our inmost selves. This is a moment of profound receptivity which, not to be equated with mere passivity, connects us with the original and originating source of all activity.

It is interesting to note that Teresa and John developed an understanding of the significance of the dark night in the midst of their intense involvement in the ecclesiastical and imperial politics of their day. In their efforts to reform the Carmelites, they often faced severe opposition from members of the hierarchy, of the ruling class, and of their own communities. However, Teresa and John were able to combine the most extraordinary activity with the deepest contemplation, writing, working and traveling extensively, even while caught up in a wordless mystical relationship with God.

The image of the dark night was used by Teresa and John and others primarily in terms of the journey of an individual toward a fuller life with God. But this same image can also be extended and re-interpreted to give us an image of a particular period in the history of a whole culture or of a specific group of people. Elie Weisel's book *Night*, for example, has provided an image of the darkness of the whole of the twentieth century in which the crucible of the Holocaust was forged. When the young Elie entered Auschwitz, all of his images of a loving God went up in the smoke of human ashes. As one enters the experience of the Holocaust through the eyes of a child, one experiences the limits of any previous explanation of the meaning of suffering.

Another contemporary novel, *Black Rain* by Masuji Ibuse, draws us into the horror that was Hiroshima. Reading this book, I felt as if my capacity to comprehend had been vaporized along with the vaporization of thousands of human beings. For those of us who live under the shadow of the mushroom cloud, the darkest of nights seems possible for us as a human race.

The image of the dark night is helpful not only in describing this moment in our culture but also in naming the present experience in most religious congregations. We are entering into a period, or have been there for some time, when previous images of religious life seem illusory and any future images are elusive. It is a moment of little knowing and even less understanding. It is difficult to see through.

Before discussing the temptations in this dark time, it should be pointed out that John of the Cross distinguished between "the dark night of the senses," which afflicts almost everyone who begins to pray, and "the dark night of the soul," which affects only those who have been seriously engaged in the process of prayer. He felt that the night of the senses had the salutary effect of weaning a person away from the deadly vices of pride, greed, lust, anger, gluttony, envy, and sloth.[2] We might wonder whether the dark night in religious life will wean us from our cultural sense of being the center of the world, from the temptation to treat persons as things, from our resentment of the limits imposed by socio-economic realities, from our desire to experience many forms of spirituality, from our cultural bias in favor of competition rather than co-operation, and from our alienation from our work.

Nevertheless, some religious today have probably also entered into the dark night of the soul. The diminishment of numbers in congregations is nothing compared to the diminishment of meaning taking place at this time. Carmelite sister Constance FitzGerald has written eloquently about the impasse and dark night being experienced by groups in the church, particularly women. "We are affected by darkness, where we are most deeply involved and committed, and in what we love and care for most."[3] The darkness deadens our desire "in the very area of life in which one is most involved and therefore most vulnerable."[4] Within religious congregations, this dark night begins with the awareness of the collapse of systems of meaning, symbolic structures, institutional cohesiveness and, most of all, relationships. "There seems no possibility of movement backward or forward," FitzGerald writes, "but only imprisonment, lack of vision, and failure of imagination."[5]

TEMPTATIONS IN THE DARK NIGHT

This dark night may or may not be articulated as such within a particular congregation. However, my work with several communities leads me to believe that most congregations experience it in one way or another. Needless to say, very few would willingly choose to pass through this dark night without some assurance that there was light at the end of the tunnel. And there are many temptations to deny or escape the reality of this searing experience. Most of these could be described as attempts to fabricate a future in the face of the unraveling of religious life in the present. I use the term "fabricate" not merely to extend the central metaphor of this book but to indicate our very human tendency to try to manufacture our own lives. We try to control through what we manufacture rather than trusting in the mysterious process of creation, which is both God's gift to us and our work. Fabrications are not suited to the life of faith. They don't wear well.

Liberals and conservatives are tempted, in different ways, to try to fabricate the future. Liberals are more tempted to expand the possibilities for the future than to choose to focus their efforts on a few projects or a limited set of options. I have discussed some of the reasons for this in the previous chapter. However, the unwillingness to make choices that would exclude some possibilities could also arise from a conscious or subconscious desire not to exclude anyone in the congregation. It is a way of trying to ensure that at least most of the members presently in the congregation will stay. This temptation seems particularly true of communities with diminishing numbers. The future of the congregation becomes even more diffuse.

The conservative temptation is to try to manufacture some sense of order in a situation they perceive as chaotic. In North America, this attempt at ordering rarely involves the blatant exercise of authority to achieve the desired result. More often than not, these conservative efforts (which can exist even within the most liberal congregations) become an attempt to order the world through paper—papering over. Many papers with guidelines, procedures, and structural precisions become the means to bring a certain order into a congregational house. This effort to order and clarify may help to conserve some of the energy unnecessarily wasted because of confusion, but it does little to revitalize a congregation. It seems mysterious but it is true that only a shared sense of vision brings real clarity and a sustained sense of direction. Visions order life from within. If we don't understand this we will continue to observe communities routinely stuffing congregational papers into drawers—to be read later. The future can be filed away.

Congregations that are more tempted by conservative illusions are more prone to elect leaders who can be counted on to follow whatever rules and procedures there are. Or they may elect those who are perceived as loyal to the tradition of the congregation, which seems a little clearer in retrospect. Or a congregation may elect a strong individual whose force of personality alone promises to bring its own kind of order. Such persons usually discover, sometimes painfully, that while they may hold office they have little real authority. Any authority based on an externalized sense of order, an appeal to tradition or definition through personality, will ultimately be weakened by its lack of reference to any larger authorizing vision or sense of purpose.

In spite of their differing attempts to fabricate a future, many liberals and conservatives share the common illusion that the future will be made through new people entering religious life. This illusion moves congregations to invest their hope for the future in the process of recruitment and formation.

There is something authentic in this hope and something healthy in the desire to share this way of life with others. There is reason to be concerned when a congregation ceases to invest an important part of its finances and energies in the process of incorporating new members. However, there may also be something inauthentic about investing all, or most, of a congregation's hope for the future in its most recent members. This overinvestment of energies can indicate that a congregation expects the process of formation to compensate for the members' inability or unwillingness to face the challenge of creating a future together.

One way of discerning the authenticity or inauthenticity of a community's concern for formation is to reflect on the quality of its response to the news of new members entering or leaving. For example, if a community is elated when one person enters and is thrown into confusion and despair when one person leaves, then that is a sign of a community that is very insecure about its future. A community attempting to fabricate a future through formation will act as if a few people entering will make a future possible, or that a few people leaving will shut off that possibility. Instead of focusing on the question of whether or how a future will be held in common, some congregations focus on the losses and gains in numbers entering and on the pluses and minuses of their formation program. Sometimes I think new members indicate less about our future and more about who we really are and where we really are now. Prospective candidates gravitate toward communities that appear to embody a similar set of values. For better or worse, they reveal us to ourselves.

Formation is frequently a flashpoint for a congregation's unresolved feelings about the future. Because of this, new members or those involved in incorporating them into the congregation suffer the consequences of a congregation's irresolution. As the crisis of religious life in North America deepens, there is an increasing amount of time, attention, and money invested in new members. The effect of this overinvestment in new members varies, depending on the circumstances of different congregations.

In some situations, new members undergo a scrutiny unknown to previous generations in religious life. This examination sometimes develops into an excessive self-examination on the part of new members, a self-preoccupation from which they may or may not recover. In other situations, a community provides the best of all possibilities for the formation of new members. Little is asked of these new members and therefore little is given. There may be a certain honesty in not demanding too much of these people. A community can hardly ask of new members what it is not willing or able to ask of those who are already professed. Self-sacrifice makes little sense if it is not in terms of some greater vision of mission which is equally served by all.

I remember being very moved by the opening scene of the film *The Mission*. A young Jesuit in an eighteenth-century Paraguayan jungle was climbing up a sheer face of rock by a waterfall to go to serve the people who had recently sent one of his brothers over the waterfall on a crucifix. I wondered: for what would I climb up a sheer face of rock and face almost certain death? For what would I ask someone else to undertake such a climb?

When a congregation lacks a compelling sense of mission, it can neither appeal to nor develop the tremendous sense of generosity in some of those initially attracted to religious life. Indeed, a community that does not expend itself for the sake of something greater will squander even the reserves of generosity within its already professed members.

A conservative congregation may ask its new members to go beyond their personal interests but it will probably be for the sake of order rather than for the sake of mission. The futility of the conservative way of coping with the dark night in religious life may or may not be felt by those in formation.

However, the dilemmas of liberalism cannot be avoided by formation teams in a more liberal congregation. They are faced with the task of preparing candidates for religious life—but which model of religious life? Within any liberal congregation there are probably many operative models of formation, regardless of the officially stated model. There are probably also many understandings of church, of ministry, of community, of the role of religious in the world. As a result, any formation model will probably be considered inherently inadequate by some congregation members. In this situation, many liberal formation teams have decided to emphasize the personal and spiritual growth of the candidates in the hope that this will provide them with a way to sustain a deeper religious identity and commitment in the midst of the diverse lifestyles and commitments open to them. In religious life, as in the culture, there is an option for personal integration in the face of a distingrating social reality. As a result, most formation personnel within liberal congregations have some background in spiritual direction or counselling. If they don't have that background they soon feel the need to get it.

Nevertheless, no matter how ambiguous the process of formation may be at this point in history, it is less ambiguous than a congregation that ceases to be concerned about new members. And there are congregations that have decided, consciously or subconsciously, to be more concerned about the future of present members. These congregations are very concerned about financial security and retirement programs. A responsible concern for aging members is important but, again, it can become unhealthy when there is an over-investment of time, money, and energy in fabricating a secure future.

There is a certain tragic illusion in such an effort. Within the broader social context, some people are beginning to realize that social security for the elderly is becoming more fragile as the number of people paying into it becomes smaller than those who are drawing on its benefits. Continuing inflation means that any economic investment in future security will follow the law of diminishing returns. A society that has chosen to restrict immigration and to have fewer children will ultimately cut off the only real basis for its own security for the elderly. Similarly, the only real security for a congregation's future lies in its future members. As I have worked with various congregations I have noticed the significant fact that the groups least worried about their financial security were those attracting a number of vocations.

These are some of the practical ways in which we are tempted to fabricate a future at this dark time. They are temptations to minimalize or to deny the depth of the problems we face. However, an even more subtle temptation arises when we attempt to face the future and reflect on it: the temptation to try to conceive (conceptualize) a future model of religious life based on an analysis of the present moment. This often results in a kind of conceptual reversal, some inversion of the present image of religious life. This conceptualizing does not lead to a new model of religious life but rather to a model that is only the flip side of an old model. Something like this went on in the heady days following Vatican II. We imagined that a new model of religious life would be the reversal of the older model. Thus, the liberal model was the reverse image of the traditional model. If the traditional model was hierarchical, the newer model would be more communal; if the traditional model was uniform, the newer would be more pluralistic, etc. This process did yield its own clarity and sense of direction.

The problem with this kind of approach is now becoming more

apparent. The clarity and sense of direction engendered through such a process lasts only as long as the more traditional model is clearly remembered. Those who have a vivid memory of the traditional model of church and religious life seem clearer about the value and significance of the liberal model of religious life. But does the liberal model make sense in itself, i.e., without reference to the more traditional model? There are those who, like myself, never knew the traditional model or never knew it for long. We know the liberal model was launched from the base of traditional religious life, but we are beginning to wonder whether there is enough fuel in the liberal model itself to take it very far. To use another metaphor, we are beginning to feel that going with a liberal model of religious life is like driving into the future through a rear-view mirror.

Thinking about the future is inevitably limited by the fact that we cannot conceive of something new except in categories of thought developed through previous experiences. Thus, it seems rather futile to try *to think* our way into the future. It would be easy to think about a future model of religious life as the reverse image of the present liberal model, but would it be worthwhile? We could think, for example, that if the liberal model is pluralistic, then a newer model would be more unified; if the present model of religious life is still quite patriarchal, then a future model must be more feminist. Maybe and maybe not. Conceptual blueprints of the future always seem to miss some of unpredictabilities even in our present reality. The future is always more original than our thinking of it. A blueprint of the future is not the same as a vision of it. Blueprints may be comforting but they may also be meaningless. What we need is vision (a *why*), not a blueprint of *what* and *how*. The crisis of religious life at this time is that the meaning that formerly constituted its world has collapsed.[6] Only a new meaning can reconstitute religious life.

Threading Our Way

Meaning is not something we can fabricate; it is something we discover. How do we discover a new meaning of religious life when a previous meaning has unraveled? Victor Frankl, the founder of logotherapy, spent his whole life exploring the dynamics of the human person's search for meaning. This desire for meaning, he said, defined a person far more than the search for pleasure or power. "Only if the original concern with meaning is frustrated do we turn to pleasure or power."[7] On the basis of his own experience of surviving in a concentration camp, he concluded that we are more pulled by meaning than pushed by the past. Human beings suffer, he said, when they are not pulled by meaning. He would say to the suffering people he counselled, "What counts is...what waits in the future, waits to be actualized by you."[8]

Victor Frankl never attempted to say *what* the meaning of a person's life should be. He simply communicated his conviction *that* there was meaning and that this meaning could be discovered by each person. He did not define meaning. He described it, bore witness to it.

How can we, in this threadbare time, discover the meaning of this moment in religious life? Following Frankl's advice and the wisdom of Teresa of Avila and John of the Cross, we can begin by trusting that there *is* meaning in this moment, even if we do not know exactly *what* it is.

We can also begin to articulate what has become meaningless in religious life. This in itself can be a meaningful activity. I learned this in the course of reviewing the novels of Elie Weisel. All his writings are marked by a refusal to give meaning to the Holocaust. This refusal arose from his deep sense of the difference between meaning and meaninglessness. Yet, in refusing to give meaning to the Holocaust, he has helped to restore some sense of what is meaningful. In marking out the limits of meaning, he has set a certain boundary to meaninglessness.[9] To name what has become meaningless in religious life is, paradoxically, to restore some faith and hope in its meaningfulness.

A trust in the possibility of meaning and a resistance to what is meaningless: these two attitudes can help us thread our way through this dark night.

There are also particular things we can do to discover those threads that will connect us to the future. A woman I directed on a retreat taught me a great deal about the mysterious relationship between activity and receptivity in our relationship to God and to the future. She was a very active feminist but she had discovered that she was curiously passive in her relationship with God: waiting for God to make it all happen and then angry when God didn't. During the retreat she received a profound grace and this is how she began to live out of it: every morning she would get up before dawn and go to a place where she could greet the dawn. She could not make the sun rise, but she could place herself where it could be seen. She was holding herself in readiness.

In the remaining sections of this chapter, I shall explore how a transformation (or conversion) of our connections to time and place can become transforming threads of the future, strands of the Spirit.

CONNECTING IN TIME

Forgiveness: Lifting the Darkness of the Past

The past hangs over many congregations like a dark cloud. Few communities have escaped the consequences of mistaken policies, the sins of power and weakness, the wounds that widen and deepen with time. The past is always problematic but it becomes even more so in times of accelerated change, such as the last twenty-five years. Times of change are inherently more conflict-ridden. The conflicts engendered by such a time are not merely the usual conflicts of personalities. There are conflicts of values and worldviews that cannot quickly be resolved without imposing the violence of compromise. Very few congregations have been able to see through some of the underlying problems posed by their decision to become more involved in the world. As a result, many of the unresolved conflicts of values have been reduced to personality conflicts. This projection of conflicts leads only to further irresolution and saps the resolve of a congregation for the future. In this moment of historical stress, is there any congregation that does not need to confess: "We have sinned against one another and against the Spirit."

As members experience the burden of the mistakes of the past, they are more likely to wonder whether the future too may be mistaken. The more a congregation becomes mired in the past, the less likely it will be to take a step into the future. A friend of mine once told me that it was only when she began to forgive her mother for her mistakes that she (my friend) could trust that her daughter would be able to forgive her whatever mistakes she was making as a mother right now. "That helped me relax about the future," said my friend.

The past, of course, cannot be undone. Forgetting or denying will not change the facts of the past. However, forgiveness can deprive the past of the power to dominate not only the present but the future as well. We sometimes live with the illusion that the past will take care of itself if we just keep moving along. It doesn't. When the past is simply left behind, it has a way of catching up with us and overtaking the present.

It would seem important, then, to develop authentic rituals of forgiveness at local and congregational levels. There are many skills developed in communities over the past few years that would seem to encourage this; two of these skills are the facilitation of dialogue and honest confrontation. However, we may have a cultural overconfidence in these skills. The liberal part of us believes that all conflicts can be managed and "worked through," salvation by interaction, which could be a long time coming. The most significant problems of the past that we share could take a lifetime to work through.

Authentic rituals of forgiveness would involve some way of saying, "I'm sorry. We're sorry." "You're forgiven. We trust we are forgiven." Beyond these words, we need an explicit resolution not to repeat the patterns of past, a firm purpose of amendment. A communal exercise of forgiveness is ultimately an act of faith in the gracious ground of our life together.

This would be an empty ritual, of course, if it were done too easily or too quickly. It could be a temptation in liberal congregations that place a high value on balancing and reconciling the various differences in a group. A minimal reconciliation would seem better than no reconciliation at all. Far from relieving the burdens of the past, though, this minimal reconciliation simply increases the illusory quality of the present. This is not peace. This is pacification. Reconciliation cannot be bought at the expense of truth and justice. It involves uncovering, not covering over. Although reconciliation involves a resolution not to dwell on the past, it does not imply denying that past.

The past darkens our present but enlightens it as well; it is not only a burden but a blessing also. Recalling the blessings of our shared past helps us to assume its burdens anew. As we transform our attitudes to our shared past, in forgiveness and gratitude, our energies are more liberated for the future.

Gratitude: Embracing the Poverty of the Present

I have suggested that we are prone to many illusions during this dark in-between time in religious life. The collapse of a previous system of meaning has made us more vulnerable to believing in the fabrications of the American empire. There are many ways to attempt to fabricate the future but the most consequential is the attempt to construct our very selves. In a declining empire, we are easily tempted by a self-development project. Identity is some *thing* to be manufactured. We try to "work on" ourselves. Relationships are to be "worked through." We engage in "dream work."

Underlying these efforts is the assumption that the self is a thing that can be put together or taken apart, something that can be constantly redesigned, something that is always in danger of becoming obsolete. We talk of finding ourselves, as if there was some *thing* we could finally possess if we could just peel away enough layers of our life to see it.

In a dark time, we are tempted to make the self our most precious possession. If our identity is thus manufactured, with what and with whom will we identify? The manufactured self is unlikely to identify itself with any future beyond its control. Once we have fabricated our identities, we almost inevitably identify ourselves with the fabrications of the empire.

If we are to become free for the future, we must discover our true identity, which is created by God rather than manufactured by us. In the dark night of these times, we need the grace of poverty of spirit (which is also the grace of gratitude) to discover our true identities. Let me explain this by describing someone I met a few years ago. He was a small and very vulnerable child with the name Christopher, the Christ-bearer. In meeting Christopher, I would discover later, I had met myself.

Christopher had long been awaited. His two parents, my friends, had already been through the sorrow of several miscarriages. Finally, it seemed as if this pregnancy would come to full term. We waited in hope. The child was born and he was called Christopher. Very soon we learned that he had a congenital defect, that his lungs would not be able to grow along with the rest of his body. He was weak. He could not see or hear or respond very well. His life, the doctors told us, would be limited to a few months.

My first reaction was one of profound sorrow for my friends, Yet, it was they who drew me beyond this sense of sorrow. Day after day, as they held his hand through the opening in the incubator, as they sang to him through the plastic walls, I could see that their hearts were more filled with love than with sorrow. While I had been focusing on the brevity of his life and his impending death, they were dwelling in a sense of gratitude for his life, for the miracle of his beginning. While I was angry at what was being taken away, they were reverencing what had been given. For them, Christopher was a gift, not a possession.

Christopher couldn't do anything for us except just be. Yet, he called forth love from our hearts. By some standards, he was slightly deformed but in our eyes he was lovely. His movements were weak and his sounds were almost silent. Yet, we knew *who* he was. His name was Christopher.

Several years after Christopher's death, I had the feeling, while on a long retreat, that my breathing was shallow, that my life was shallow. I felt the need to breathe deeply, to be inspired. Spiritually, I was gasping for air. At that moment, I felt the presence of Christopher, the Christ-bearer, once more in my life. At that moment, I felt that I *was* Christopher, that Christopher was the deepest truth of my life. Carl Jung would have called this an awareness of my "Christ-self."

I experienced my life as a miracle of creation. I understood that God looked on me as we had looked on Christopher: with love. God's love was there not because of anything I did, or how I looked, or why I responded. This was at once the grace of poverty of spirit and gratitude. In a moment of utter simplicity I knew who I was, just as I knew who Christopher was. My identity is that I am of God, with God, for God. This identity, as Thomas Merton has tried to describe it, is beyond all social fabrications:

> At the center of my being is a point of pure nothingness which is untouched by sin and by illusion, a point of pure truth, a point or spark which belongs entirely to God, which is never at our disposal, from which God disposes of our lives, which is inaccessible to the fantasies of our own mind or the brutalities of our own will. This little point of nothingness and of absolute poverty is the pure glory of God in us.[10]

When we discover this identity, as individuals and as communities, we are more likely to trust in the future as "as point of pure truth...which is inaccessible to the fantasies of our own mind or the brutalities of our own will." When we know who we truly are, we can trust who we shall be. In discovering that we do not possess ourselves in the present, we can allow ourselves to be possessed by hope for the future. Gratitude is the grounding in the present that connects us with the deepest point of our lives and the furthest point of our future. Just being in the darkness of this in-between desert time is not a bad place to be when we know the goodness of just being.

As religious communities, we need rituals to celebrate our sense of gratitude for our shared life. We need the appropriate symbols and activites that deepen our communal sense of gratitude. We need times when we do more than calculate the pluses and minuses of our common life, when we stop doing a cost-benefit analysis of our shared future. There are small moments to be seized: birthdays, jubilees, the day we found what was lost, the day just before all the other days in our lives. In the long-haul struggle to see religious life through these times and into the future, we often lose sight of the distant shore of our desire. We need to set down small islands of hope through celebrations to help us keep sight of that distant shore.

Within the Catholic tradition, two sacraments have signified the conversion of our stance to the past and the present: reconciliation and the eucharist. These sacraments seem more necessary than ever during this dark time. Unfortunately, they have never seemed more problematic, especially to female religious. Women are realizing how much these liberating sacraments have also served to reinforce a patriarchal structure in the church. This experience has moved some women to develop their own rituals of cleansing and celebration. The inherent ambiguity in this effort is that significant symbols cannot be manufactured or constructed; they can be transformed and re-interpreted, but they cannot be fabricated.

Religious, and not only women religious, must find some "resourcement" for these times, i.e., "the creative engagement with the received Catholic symbols in dialectical effort both to break them open to new purposes, experiences and questions and to allow these latter, in turn, to challenge the tradition."[11] We are held so captive in this culture that only sacraments and symbols that connect us deeply to the long and deep power of the liberating Spirit can free the energy we so need at this moment. We need more than the prepackaged liturgies that are found in many parishes, and more than the throw-away rituals of ad hoc groups.

CONNECTING PLACES

In order to discover meaning in a dark time, we need to discover those places that help us to position ourselves, as it were, for the future. As Christians we believe that every space in life is open to the future. Nevertheless, the evidence of history suggests that some spaces are more open to the future than others. Our challenge is to discern where those spaces are now. There has been a great deal written in recent years on various methods of discernment, on the *how* of discernment. Although this has been most helpful, we need to reflect more on the *where* of discernment.

Where does discernment of the future best take place? Where should we place ourselves so that the future may present itself? Where does the future claim us as its own?

Placing Ourselves in Prayer

If we grant that a vision, a shared vision, of the future must be discovered rather than constructed, where will it come from? It will come from the deepest level of our lives, from the level where our communion with God coincides with our community with others. Thomas Merton called this the level of the "true self," where the self draws closer to others as it draws closer to God.[12] This level of life is far deeper than the conscious levels on which we usually live (the levels of the psychological or the social self). On our conscious or self-conscious levels, we tend to fabricate, to project, to move between clarity and illusion. However, visions come from that more than conscious level which is beyond our control. From this deepest level, visions emerge—sometimes in the form of dreams.

Fortunately, there is an increasing interest in North America in the significance of dreams. Unfortunately, the appreciation of dreams is often confined to an individual or therapeutic process. While this may help an individual discover a personal vision, it is less likely to reveal a shared vision that constitutes shared life and action. A common vision is more than the sum of the private dreams of the individuals who call themselves a community. Our question then becomes: How can a community place itself in a position to discover the common vision that lies in the depths of shared life?

This question leads me to consider that one of the most important purposes of being together in community is to be together in prayer. This implies far more than "shared prayer," which often tends to move on a more conscious level. Being together in prayer first involves encouraging each other in the inward journey to the level of the true self where we are what we truly are: beyond all our social roles and our psychologically predictable patterns. To be together in prayer we must confirm each other in our solitude. This is a challenge for community in a culture that tends to flee from solitude to superficial togetherness or to the illusions the self can harbor in isolation. We live in a psychologically conscious culture that makes us more comfortable talking about ourselves but less comfortable about dwelling in silence at the deeper level of our existence.

One example of this being together in prayer is the Quaker meeting where people come together for an hour to be together in prayer. In silence, they try to attune themselves to the "inner light" within each person and within the group. Even if the meeting ends without a word being spoken, it is, nonetheless, a prayer meeting. Sometimes out of the shared silence a word takes shape, a prayer is breathed. However, it does not matter if or when these spiritual shoots break the surface of the silence. What matters is more than the words, more than the silence itself. I remember sitting in a Quaker prayer meeting and thinking, "This is a space in which visions are born."

This kind of shared silence may also be an appropriate form of prayer for communities who have "named" their experience of the dark night. It is a way of being together in the darkness, in the unknowing, in the silence. It is an act of believing that there is light—within each person and between persons—even if we do not yet know exactly what the light is. This form of prayer engages, rather than escapes, the reality of this dark time.

However, this kind of prayer must always be nourished by the symbols and stories of our faith. We live in a culture that so stimulates our imaginations that our souls are left too numb for visions. Consumerism leaves us with a craving, not for visions but for illusions. Our imaginations are stunted, our hearts weakened, and our souls shrunken to a shadow of our truer selves. What passes for "vision" at numerous conferences across the land is often nothing more than the latest formula for survival. We need to nourish an alternative imagination, which is what the stories in Scripture are all about. A friend of mine, who works with native people, explained this to me rather simply: "Sometimes it feels as if there is no hope against the Goliaths of this world. And then I read Scripture and I remember that sometimes the Davids win."

The frequent reading of the stories of Scripture, or the frequent recitation of the psalms, plants them (through repetition) in the ground of our subconscious. It is there, on this level, that these stories merge with our story and transform it from within. A space opens within from where we discover the possibility of co-authoring a vision which is authoritative.

The stories of Scripture were co-authored in the sense that they emerged from within the experience of a people. Their vision, which called them to be together and to act together as a people for the sake of the world, grew out of being together and acting together with God. That biblical vision has become authoritative for us today. When the stories of our ancestors in the faith merge with our story, we can become the co-authors of a biblical vision today.

When we pray together, in silence or through the words of Scripture, we hold ourselves in readiness for a vision. Perhaps we need to reflect more on the conditions that create the readiness and the willingness for visions. Visions are more easily recognized when they are awaited, longed for, and expected. If community is only functional, a base of mutual support for ministry or personal growth, we will probably be content with a functional future. At the functional level of existence we may become co-workers, co-ministers, co-inhabitants, or co-members, but we will not become co-authors of a vision for the future.

Placing Ourselves on the Periphery

By being together in prayer we center our lives in God and are drawn together to that deep place where visions emerge. Through this centering we draw on a power and an energy that is closer to us than we are to ourselves, but different enough to make us more than ourselves.

However, there is another, equally significant way we can position ourselves to discover the future. We can take our place with those on the periphery of the empire, those who are powerless because of their distance from the centers of imperial power. That distance may be marked out by geography, economic disparity, social inequality, sexual or racial discrimination. There are peripheral people within the United States and there are peripheral people in the peripheral colonies of the empire, e.g., the poor of El Salvador. These are the people who know in their bones the disintegrating effects of the realities of a declining empire. These are the people whose future is most denied by the absence of a common social vision which would connect the threads of their lives with others. Unlike the liberals (who tend to have more economic resources), the people on the periphery cannot afford the luxury of personal development or the satisfactions of personal ambition. Unlike the conservatives, they can take little consolation in efforts to put more order into society. Those on the periphery are usually the ones the conservatives define as disorderly.

The people on the periphery are living through a socio-cultural dark night. Some become, quite literally, people of the night: prostitutes, the cleaners of office buildings, and the scavengers of back alleys. Their present is more defined by the patterns of the past (whether personal or social) than by any hope of the future.

There are many and various groups whose lives have become peripheral in North America: the native peoples, the elderly, illegal immigrants, the mentally handicapped, the illiterate, some groups of women, the rural poor. One could go on. In every part of the continent, and in other countries as well, there are those who in their bodies and hearts and minds are witnesses to the bankruptcy of the illusions of America. Whether they are conscious of the cause of their suffering or not, they bear witness to the great distance between the noble ideals of the republic and the harsh reality of the empire. Perhaps this is why the powers in the empire would prefer to keep these people out of sight and out of mind. The dispirited lives on the periphery reveal the dearth of social inspiration in the empire.

Those who live inside the periphery of power in the empire—the relatively comfortable middle class—are less revealing about the decay at the center of the empire. At least until recently, they lived largely within the periphery of social power.[13] This is not to deny the very real suffering within the periphery of power. The distress of family breakups, the stress of mortgaged lives, the crises provoked by various additions—these are real sufferings. However, these problems are often seen only as individual or familial problems and the recommended solution usually takes the form of psychological treatment.

It is important, however, for people to see through these problems, to see them as symptoms of a deeper social problem. The consumption of personal relationships and the short-term nature of many relationships are examples of the problems created by the crisis of liberal capitalism. The real solution to these problems lies not only on the personal-psychological level but also on the socio-political level. Those who live within the periphery of power are not likely to raise radical questions about the basic structure and general drift of the empire. Although they feel somewhat distant from the centers of power, they also feel distant from those who live on the edge of the empire. Those who live within the periphery do not feel very powerful, but neither do they feel powerless. They can cope.

As religious, we must examine our place within the circles of power in the empire. If we stay well within the circle of power, we will be more tempted to feel that we can go on coping. Liberals or conservatives, we will find our way of coping. Within the circle of power, we will be more tempted to believe the future is ours to fabricate. Thus placed, we will keep on keeping on. We will not see the need for a new vision of religious life.

At the periphery of power, in places darkened by the shadow of the empire, religious are more likely to feel the need, the hunger, and thirst for a different kind of future. From this place, one is more likely to begin to see through the empire and to want to see the Reign of God through.

Historically, the periphery or the desert or the frontier is the place where religious congregations were founded.[14] Founders, male and female, of apostolic communities felt their hearts and souls stretched by some group, some people, some concern that was peripheral to a particular society. They went to the periphery where others would not or could not go. There they founded a community with a way of life that would make a peripheral social reality the central concern of their lives. The cries of suffering and the songs of hope of people on the periphery have always called forth new visions of religious life. But we cannot hear those cries and songs, we cannot attune ourselves to them, unless we place ourselves with those on the periphery of the empire. One could read the founding stories of many apostolic congregations as the stories about a moment when a vision was born out of a new way of being with God and a new way of being with others. In this founding moment, the experience of being deeply centered in God coincided with the experience of being called to the periphery of society.

Now, as then, religious who live and work on the periphery know the people there and call them by name. These people are not objects of social concern but persons who are seen as anything but peripheral. Now, more than ever, religious need to be with these people, not only for their sakes but for our sakes as well. We need to learn to see through their eyes, however glazed and weakened, in order to see through the reality of the time and place that is called America. From the periphery, we can begin to see the vast distance that separates the empire not only from the ideal of the republic but also from the reality of the Reign of God. On the periphery, says Brazilian theologian Leonardo Boff, the structures of empire seem most questionable and therefore in need of restructuring.

> What specifically is the place of religious in the world? It is precisely in the place where the world feels itself called into question and experiences scandal, and thus where the world experiences itself as being transcended. The poor are the ones who occupy this place....In the presence of the poor, society senses its limitations and is called to open itself and restructure itself so there is no longer any room for the exploitation of one person by another or for manipulative techniques.[15]

Some religious men and women are beginning to move toward placing their lives in solidarity with those who live on the periphery. There are those who see such a move as consistent with the founding charism of their congregation, while others see this move as consistent with their own personal sense of vocation. In any case, it is possible that something new and promising will be born as religious live on the periphery. Just possible. Not inevitable. We cannot predict what new forms of religious life will be born and which ones will die on the periphery. We cannot anticipate which of the present models of religious life will flourish anew and which ones will wither on the periphery. Time will tell. All that can be said is that on the periphery, with peripheral people, a more promising future is most needed and most wanted. It is, therefore, the place where what is promising may be more recognized and welcomed.

Placing Ourselves on Pilgrimage

There is yet a third way we can place ourselves more readily for the future, the way of pilgrimage. Some may find this a strange suggestion; indeed, I have not seen the way of pilgrimage suggested in various other writings on the future of religious life. Yet, there are many who have undertaken a pilgrimage of one sort or another in Canada and the United States today. We want to go and see those places where "good things are happening."

There is a long tradition in Christianity and in other great world religions of going on pilgrimage. This ancient practice may have a particular relevance at this time. In former days, people journeyed to holy places. Today, it is important to journey to those places that seem to hold some promise for the future. It is not enough to face the darkness of this time or to resist the illusory lights of this culture; we must also move toward discovering the deeper light—wherever that is given. While it is important to see through the patterns of the declining empire, it is also important to see where the Reign of God is growing among us even now. As Christians we believe that there is no darkness that is absolute, no darkness without its moments of light.

The process of pilgrimage involves a passing over to a new experience and a return to one's own experience.[16] Pilgrimage involves a dislocation that may help us to find our true location, our vocation, in life. Let me say it again: when we go on pilgrimage we become, by choice, displaced persons; we leave our usual place of life or work and go to a place that is holy, i.e., both fascinating and fearful.[17] We do not stay in this holy place, but if the pilgrimage has been authentic, we cannot return to our same old place in the same old way.

What would it mean for a congregation to go on pilgrimage? It would probably not mean cutting everyone loose and sending them out to wander in the desert of these times. It could mean sending out small groups to investigate the rumors of oases in the desert. It could imply welcoming the insights of those who have already undertaken such a pilgrimage on their own. It could involve a corporate reflection on the reports of those who have gone on pilgrimage.

If we want to engage in the process of reweaving religious life, we need to discover those strands in the present moment that will connect us to the future.

In placing ourselves together in prayer, together on the periphery, and together on pilgrimage, we position ourselves to discover a new meaning for religious life in this threadbare time. What that new meaning is remains to be revealed. In the next chapter, I shall describe some of my own experiences of those places in which I have discovered some of the strands of the Spirit that may connect religious life to the future. It is my conviction that it is too soon to define a new meaning for religious life. For the time being, we can only define it partially by describing our experiences of meaning, the moments of meaning that are revelatory in however fleeting a way.

"For you who walk
there is no road.
The road is made by walking."
Antonio Marchado

"Possibility and limitation
mean about the same thing."
Flannery O'Connor

"Great ideas, it has been said,
come into the world
as gently as doves.
Perhaps, then,
if we listen attentively,
we shall hear amid the uproar
of empires and nations
a faint flutter of wings,
a gentle stirring of life and hope."
Albert Camus

"Something which has existed since the beginning
that we have heard,
and we have seen with our own eyes;
that we have watched
and touched with our hands:
the Word, who is life—
this is our subject."
1 John 1:1

CHAPTER FOUR

STRANDS OF THE SPIRIT

The future of religious life depends on the process of discerning the strands of the Spirit in the midst of this threadbare moment. This process, called "reading the signs of the times" at Vatican II, urges a discernment that is far easier said than done. The methods of discernment, part of the rich tradition of the church, have tended to take the individual as the primary point of departure. In the Ignatian model of discernment, for example, the "movements" within the person and the various feelings associated with them served to identify what was of the Spirit and what was not. More recent efforts in Ignatian spirituality have tried to articulate a communal model of discernment based on the "movements" within a small group. Efforts to articulate a more political model of discernment have attempted to identify the characteristics of political realities that would most embody the values of the Kingdom of God. In Latin America and elsewhere, the poor are seen as the privileged locus for discerning political realities.

The process of discernment presumed in this chapter draws on all these models. However, I also presume that we have certain "root experiences" in our lives—radical experiences (*radix*=root)— which thread our lives together with the people of God, those now living and those who have gone before us.[1] In this chapter I will share some of my root experiences of being with others in prayer, being with others on the periphery, and being with others on pilgrimage. There are times and places when I have seen and felt some of the strands of the Spirit that could be significant in the process of reweaving religious life. I cannot *define* these strands of the Spirit in any complete or clear way, but I can *describe* them and the process of discovering them. In order to do this, I will shift to a storytelling mode. In this in-between time, when we no longer have a larger shared story, it is ever more necessary to share our stories. These stories are inevitably limited by my own experience, but to the extent that they are true stories they may provide others with a way of connecting to their own present reality and future possibilities. My hope is that these stories will encourage others to seek to discern the strands of the Spirit in their own personal or congregational stories.

PRAYER IN THE NEVADA DESERT

In May 1987, over three hundred Catholics from the United States (and many other countries) gathered at the Nevada test site to mark the fifth anniversary of the American bishops' pastoral letter on peace. We gathered to pray and to protest. I had been asked to share some reflections prior to the civil disobedience action.

My reflections began to take shape as I allowed the desert space to open my heart and mind. It attuned me to this dark and desert time we live in. We had learned about the huge craters left by the underground nuclear tests, and heard about (but were prevented from seeing) the sea of glass created as the heat of nuclear explosions dissolved the desert stones.

There are hundreds of holes of oblivion in the desert where even the stones cannot cry out.

I felt as if I was praying in the empire's heart of darkness. My soul shrank at the horror of it all and seemed to become like a small and insignificant grain of sand. I probably would have melted in the heat of those days, were it not for the knowlege that others were praying with me in this heart of darkness.

These reflections, which I shared then and do now, arose from my contemplative experience in the desert:

Like the people of Israel, like Jesus, we are being led into the desert, not to escape but rather to confront our illusions. The desert is where we are tempted by mirages, where truth is put to the test. Like the early desert mothers and fathers, we are being led into the wilderness to test not only our personal illusions but also the social illusions of the declining American empire....The illusions of this declining empire are structured into this society in the most elusive way. Anyone who works for justice and peace knows this even before they name it. Once you feel the consequences of distant decisions, in terms of their impact on people's lives, you begin to ask, "Who's responsible for this misery?"

This question leads into a world structured in circles—from door to door, desk to desk. As you move back and forth between the inner and outer circles of the structure, you keep circling around the question of responsibility. It is a dizzying round of denial. Nobody seems responsible....And the problem with a situation in which nobody seems responsible is that everyone feel guilty, but only vaguely so.

We are all enveloped into the folds of the empire's elusive structures; we are encircled by its fictions....We are not up against a good old-fashioned hierarchical structure in which there are clear, but often unjust, lines of responsibility and accountability. We are encircled by structures that enshroud the manufacture of mass death....

Let us see through the illusions of this empire without lapsing into our own delusions. Ronald Reagan, for example, was neither the savior of the empire nor its demon. Reagan was an illusion. But illusions are powerful. Illusions are dangerous.

In this desert time, we are called to resist the illusions of the empire; yet, a clear response to this call often eludes us. In the long struggle with the evasions of justice, we can become like what we are fighting against. We are prone to self-delusion. We can become elusive to ourselves. What then? What now?

The road to resisting the illusions of a desert time lies by way of the facts. Which facts? Not simply more facts about the horrors of global holocaust. It seems that the more facts we know about nuclear weapons, the less we feel able to do. No, not this way.

We need to recover an even more basic fact, the fact of life itself. Our resistance to the illusions of a dying empire begins with life, with amazement at the fact of simply being alive. Our resistance to the elusive structures that enshroud the organization of death begins with a sense of awe about the fact of having been born.

We tend to take the fact of our life for granted. Yet, how easily the slightest change in our parents' circumstances could have resulted in the birth of someone, but not the person who is alive now. "We ain't necessarily so." There is all the difference in the world between being born and not being born. To dwell on this difference, to delight in it, is to open ourselves to the revelation that life is a gift. To contemplate this most obvious fact reveals the root of our religious resistance....

The desert is that space in our lives where we are called to resist the illusions that make life or death fictitious, where we must resist the mirages that blur the difference between life and death. The desert is that time in our lives when we act on the fact of our lives, when we become a factor in history.

However, the desert is not only a place of resistance; it is also the moment in which we discern what should not be resisted. The desert is the stretching space of our lives in which we encounter God as the irresistible One. Life and love and beauty and truth are the almost irresistible moments of manna in these desert times. Yet, we are sometimes more tempted to resist love and life than we are to accept violence and war. At those times, we reinforce our self-illusions and resist becoming who we really are: people for whom the bottom line of life is a blessing. Our resistance to illusions is only as tough as our willingness to surrender to the irresistible reality of grace in our lives.[2]

Through this experience of prayer in the desert, I discovered a strand of the Spirit that may become part of the process of reweaving religious life. This strand ties us to the Spirit of creation.

Our amazement at the miracle of our own beginnings draws us closer to the God of beginnings and to our own power to begin something new in the midst of an aging empire. There is a profound connection between the prayer of gratitude, addressed to the God of beginnings, and our belief in our political capacity to initiate something new in the world and in the church.

FROM THE PERIPHERY: STORIES FROM EL SALVADOR

Not long ago, I spent some time in El Salvador with a group of Americans who went to support the Salvadoran refugees who wanted to return to their homes in that country. We heard many stories. Somehow, they have become part of our story.

There are children in El Salvador who grow up learning the facts of death before they learn the facts of life. One such child is the son of Miguel Angela Montenegro, a leader in the Human Rights Commission of El Salvador (CDHES).

The son wandered into the documentation room as Miguel was showing us the evidence of human rights abuse in that country. The commission's work of the previous day had already been developed into photographs and recorded on videotape. There, in black and white and color, were the bodies of two young men: one had been decapitated, his testicles mutilated. The other showed different signs of torture: the fingers of his right hand were cut off. As I gasped, Miguel's young son began to look at the photos on the table. The father made no attempt to hide this brutal reality from him.

Early childhood educators elsewhere may shudder at this. Neuroses. Psychoses. Not nice, not healthy, not happy. What will this child grow up to be? If he becomes the man his father is, he will become a Christian.

Miguel, compact and clear, was a revelation to me of the depths of the Christian mystery being lived out in El Salvador. Somehow, he has gone beyond his fear of death. Because he has died before he dies, he has become one of the liberators in this land dominated by the terror of death.

On the walls of CDHES, in the modest two-story house that is both home and office to members of the commission, are the photos of seven other members of the organization who have been assassinated since its founding in 1978. One of the photos is of Dr. Marianella Garcia Villas, president of the commission until her assassination in March 1983. Her tortured body was found completely dismembered. "It was Marianella who got me involved in the commission," says Miguel. The most recent photo is of Herbert Anaya Sanabria, murdered in October 1987 while taking his children to school. The words below the photo develop a picture of Anaya's soul: "The agony of not working for justice is stronger than the certain possibility of my death; this latter is but one instant; the other is one's whole life."

Miguel carries on, taking up the refrain of those now silenced. For him, as for others, death is a certain possibility, not death from natural causes but death deliberately organized and executed. Most of Miguel's relatives have been murdered. He has already been arrested and tortured and he has received numerous death threats. Friends and supporters have offered him airfare out of the country and a safe place for his family, his wife, and four young children.

"I am sick and tired of threats against my life," he says. "We will continue our work." Why? How? "People come to us and ask us not to abandon them. Those who suffer fill us with strength and hope. We know we are not alone. We are confident you will not leave us alone."

We wonder if he is afraid. "Are we afraid? Of course we are afraid. Every human being is afraid of dying. But if we are ruled by fear we will do nothing."

The whole military and political apparatus in El Salvador rules by fear. Terror tactics take many forms: harassment of civilians, the military "operations," the destruction of property, the destruction of body and soul through torture. It works—but not always. Sometimes, in some places, in some people, death no longer has dominion. There are those who, like Miguel, have *lived* their fear until the fear blinked at life.

The desire to live freely and meaningfully robs death of its power. For some, like Miguel, a *chosen* death is preferable to mute submission to the murderous machinery of terror. Such a choice promises liberation not only for oneself but also for others. It is a resurrecting choice, one that was made by Archbishop Oscar Romero, whose spirit still hovers over this land. Two weeks before his murder, he said, "I have often been threatened with death, but as a Christian, I do not believe in death without resurrection. If they kill me, I will rise in the Salvadoran people."

Romero's hope in the resurrection is echoed by many who face certain death in El Salvador. Their faith in the power of the Spirit is matched by their belief that they are part of a community of struggle. "If I die," says one health-care worker, "another will take my place."

The words of this person, of Miguel, of Herbert Anaya and Oscar Romero speak of deep freedom; they are the words of those who are free to live and free to die. There is a great deal of propaganda about "freedom" in El Salvador. In the name of democratic freedoms, the United States has been pouring more than one million dollars a day into this country to prop up the facade of freedom. In reality, this "freedom" is merely license for the few. Sometimes it becomes a license to kill.

Nevertheless, the cycle of fear, of destruction and degradation, is broken by those liberators who have died before they die. Their resurrection and that of their people begins even now. Marx was only partly right when he criticizied the religious belief in life after life as "the opium of the people." There are times and places when only a life directed by faith in some kind of resurrection can liberate people from the domination of death.[3]

I discovered a strand of the Spirit with these people on the periphery of the empire. It could be deeply significant in the process of reweaving religious life; it ties us to God who is Redeemer. Somehow we need to reclaim a sense of religious life as a way of dying before we die and to understand the vows as a way of liberating us from the claims and securities of the present, for the sake of the future. Perhaps this is simply another way of saying that religious life is an eschatological sign, a way of beginning to live an alternative future, even now in the midst of the empire.

ON PILGRIMAGE: THE SIDE ROADS OF AMERICA

As 1987 began, my insights into the decline of the American empire had been brought to the front burner of my consciousness
where I kept it at a slow simmer. I searched for some way to discover whether there was anything of the Spirit growing in this
time of cultural decline. As I traveled throughout the United
States and Canada, I began to ask, "Where do you see signs of the
Spirit?" It was, I thought, the kind of open-ended question that
could have led anywhere: to persons, to movements, to books, to
programs. In fact, the question took me to very out of the way
places: to the cornfields of the midwest, through Appalachia, up
into the Great Smoky Mountains of North Carolina, and onto
those roads in Wisconsin and Minnesota where deer warnings
abound.

This kind of question, I realize, yields neither the kind of statistics necessary for a sociological survey nor the collection of facts
required by investigative journalism. Nevertheless, stated in such
theological terms, it does unfold the kind of revelation that can
happen on a pilgrimage.

I put this question to many people who were neither very rich
nor very poor, at gatherings of every sort. They were somewhat
educated, concerned about the church (even if not actively involved in it), largely Catholic (although not exclusively so), more
to the left than the right. It was a sampling of people with views
not unlike those of the readership of *Catholic New Times* or the *National Catholic Reporter*. In one sense, you could say that I was relying on what has been called (in the tradition of the church) the
"sensus fidelium," the consensus of the faithful. I simply presumed that it was worthwhile exploring what a number of people
sensed as significant signs of the Spirit. Such a sampling is limited
and any reflections that follow upon it will also be limited. It
seemed like a good place to start. These people, at least, understood the question.

The question they were asked could have led them to, through,
or beyond the church. It left them free to identify the Reign of
God with the empire or to distinguish between them. As the

responses began to accumulate, I took note of those places mentioned by a significant number of people: there were houses of prayer, pastoral programs for Hispanics in the Southwest and native peoples in the north, resistance communities in large urban centers on both coasts, creation-centered rural communities, houses of welcome and mercy, projects in socio-economic transformation, old and new monastic communities—all scattered over Canada and the United States. (Later I would learn that the places not mentioned were as significant as those that were.)

Given my limited time, I chose to focus first on a region I knew the least—the Midwest United States and Appalachia—because I wanted to be open to patterns of thought and action other than my usual ones. My reflections are doubtless influenced by the peculiarities of these regions. In consequence, this report is not only interim but also partial; it is more invitational than conclusive. Nevertheless, what I learned on this pilgrimage seems significant. Some of the insights that emerged along the way have proved helpful in elucidating various situations I have observed in other parts of the United States and Canada.

Here is an interim report from the side roads of America.

I was surprised how I was invariably directed off the main roads to the side roads of America (those poorly marked roads where the strands of the Spirit may be found) as I followed the responses to the question, "Where do you see signs of the Spirit?" My companion on the journey was a sister from Costa Rica. Each of us had a certain perspective that comes from living in one of the empire's colonies. We wanted to see how things appeared in the empire itself. As the miles wore on, and as we were drawn along the byways, it became evident that we were being drawn into another angle of vision, another way of being. Each evening we spent some time reflecting on the significance of what we had heard and seen that day.

There is something rather comfortable, we realized, about life on the highways. There is the round-the-clock security of well-lit signs, gas stations and convenience stores that are always open.

Fast-food places offer sustenance and solace. You can go a long way with such ever-present conveniences and really think you are going somewhere. You can go very fast to anywhere without ever having to ask for help to get there.

Bumping along the byways is quite another experience. The signs are so few and far between that you can easily get lost—until you learn to ask for help, until you realize that everything is a potential sign. In the strangeness of dark paths, you have to go much slower so as not to miss any of the signs. You really have to want to get where you are going.

Early in this pilgrimage I became conscious of how much in this culture conspires to keep us, literally and metaphorically, on the highways, in the mainstream of things. It takes an enormous amount of effort to make the time or find the reason for taking the road less traveled. Yet, as I discovered, there are a significant number of people in America who have turned onto some side road in search of the Spirit.

If there was a kind of revelation in the course of this little pilgrimage, it was not in this or that place but in the in-between of the various experiences.

An Integrated Alternative

Between the various points of difference, there was something similar about all of the places we visited: they were all, as a sociologist would say, counter-cultural. A religious person might say that they were places where the resistance to the empire was at once an embrace of the Kingdom. Significantly, this resistance/embrace was characteristic of every dimension of life in the places we journeyed to. These were not places that were counter-cultural in one area of life and mainstream in other areas of life, but were places where people attempted an integrated way of living, praying, and acting. This integrated option seemed all the more possible on the side roads of America.

This possibility took on concrete dimensions for me in one of the first places we visited, the Quaker community in Celo, North Carolina. This community has staked out a Christian option on a land trust in the beautiful Great Smoky Mountains in the middle of nowhere, as some would think. The thirty families who live on this land trust and the other 120 people who live around it have tried to modify all the mainstream social and cultural values associated with the liberal capitalist belief in private property. The land is held in trust by the whole community but may be used by families or individuals. They may build their own homes but must sell these back to the community if they leave the land trust. A woman who calls herself "a refugee from Boston" told me that there are similar land trusts in parts of Massachusetts.

This co-operative way of living was reflected in several projects run by members of the Celo community: a preschool staffed and sponsored by parents; a junior high school in which students and teachers live together, each doing his or her share of the work necessary to keep the school going; a craft co-operative; a printing and food co-op.

Over the years, the community has developed an informal exchange economy. For example, someone teaches another's children in exchange for food or a piece of artwork. This kind of economic alternative demands and encourages a transformation of the social relationships among the members of the community. There was a conscious resistance to the relationships of competition, manipulation, and domination so characteristic of a capitalist society. In Celo, there was a genuine appreciation for the diversity of gifts in the community. Some of the gifts would seem unproductive or useless in the mainstream culture of consumerism. The community, for example, provided room and board as a way of supporting its own storyteller. A similar arrangement was made for a woman who provided a "spiritual presence" and assistance for members of the community in times of grief. One of the older couples at Celo, Dot and Bob Barrus, told us stories about what many people did to integrate their retarded daughter as a contributing member of the community. There was always room at Celo for those who would be rejected as useless in a productivity-oriented culture.

This community was not just a mutual self-development project; these people also sponsor a publication called *The Southern Rural Voice for Peace*. Celo has become a center for the peace movement in the rural south. It is also a sanctuary for refugees from Central America.

The community, which is composed of members from many denominations, gathers each Sunday morning in the tiny log meeting house for prayer in the Quaker tradition. This is the only prayer gathering of the week because, as one woman explained, "We don't really need to spend more time in prayer because we have tried to shape our whole weekday life according to what we believe in." The global concern of this community was evident in the notices posted on the meeting place door. One was the latest update on the Oscar Arias peace plan for Central America.

The transformation of weekday life by counter-culture and religious values was evident in a meeting the Celo community held to discuss the local school board elections. As concerned members of the community gathered in a circle, the discussion was guided by two principles from the Quaker tradition: a respect for "the inner light" within each person, and the testing of that "light" within the context of community.

There were many artists and craftspersons in the Celo community. One of them was Beckie, the potter. We arrived at her house just as she was finishing a clay sculpture which depicted her vision of the shape and substance of the community at Celo. She had fashioned an ark out of clay, with many people and animals in it. The persons at the top of it held up their hands in a way that made them the candle holders. "These are the older and wiser people at Celo," said Beckie. "They call us to be true to the light." She went on to say that the community at Celo was like the ark which "helps us to keep afloat and safe in a culture in which we could easily drown."

One of the members of the Celo community makes it his business to collect information on rural communities throughout the United States. He estimated that there are 10,000 rural community experiments in the country, mostly in North Carolina, the Ozarks, Appalachia, parts of New England, upstate New York, and northern California. These are among the regions where land is still available at a moderate price. Not all of these experiments are places where the Spirit is to be found. Yet, the desire that fosters so many of these rural community experiments is significant in itself.

What seemed most significant about Celo is that it has been going for over fifty years. Given the brief lifespan of many counter-cultural efforts, Celo's longevity seems worth reflecting on.

I left Celo with a sense of what an integrated way of life would look like: a coherence of political commitments, religious values, economic arrangements, social structures, and artistic expression. It struck me that this coherent way of life had become almost impossible within the disintegrating reality of mainstream America. This was why those who were looking for a more integrated way of life had moved onto the side roads; they had more of a chance to create their own alternative to the dominant patterns and values of the empire. One younger couple at Celo explained that they had moved there "to find a way of living beyond the schizophrenic existence that results from trying to live as Christians within a capitalistic culture."

Living on a side road did not prevent the people at Celo from relating to the broader society and being active within it. They were not disconnected from the social concerns of America. However, their place on a side road provided them with an integrated and alternative way of life in which to sustain their resistance to the empire.

As we drove down the winding mountain road from Celo, I thought of how many alternative projects and groups I had been part of that no longer existed. It was not surprising, I mused, because our so-called alternative had usually involved only one dimension of our lives. Sooner or later, the internal contradictions generated by trying to change one aspect of life while leaving the others unchanged began to wreak their own havoc.

I recalled my own puzzlement about the fragility of so many of the newer ventures (in lifestyle or ministry) of religious communities. After our visit to Celo, I began to realize how many of these ventures were one-dimensional: a radical effort in social justice that was not matched by a similar radicalization of prayer or community life; a wonderful renewal in spirituality that was soon consumed by the demands of productivity or even by the professionalization of prayer; an attempt to foster deeper relationships that left unquestioned the superficiality of common prayer and the dissipation of apostolic energies.

Celo was an example to me of how, in a disintegrating culture, the only real alternatives are those involving an integration of all dimensions of life. It also made me more aware of the significance of economics in developing alternatives to a culture shaped by liberal capitalism. This is not usually considered in articles about the future of religious life. Although the vow of poverty is inherently counter-cultural in its commitment to the common ownership of goods, there are a thousand ways in which many religious congregations remain tied to the dominant mode of economic life. Whether through various institutional commitments or through the demands of professional work or as beneficiaries of social securities, religious remain connected to the socio-economic system of the empire.

It would be unrealistic to imagine that we could ever live completely outside our present socio-economic system. Yet, it might be worthwhile to reflect on whether we are overly connected to the system of liberal capitalism and to what extent this keeps us tied to life on the highways of America. If religious are to be involved in shaping an alternative to the empire, one of the challenges would be whether we can begin to shape a new economic order within our own congregations.

We saw another example of an integrated alternative to the empire when we visited the Benedictine community in Erie, Pennsylvania. As we talked to various members of the community, we noticed how often they referred to the significance of their decision to make a corporate commitment to peace. The reality of this commitment was evident everywhere. Every building associated with the monastery has a sign "nuclear free zone" displayed prominently. The community's commitment to peacemaking involves organizing, publications, active civil disobedience, and countless other tasks. The Benedictines have provided the space and the personnel for the national headquarters of Pax Christi U.S.A. Students from the nearby school run by the Benedictines work as volunteers in the office. In a very real way, Erie has become the center of the Catholic peace movement in the U.S.A.

As part of its commitment to peace, the community sponsors a soup kitchen called Emmaus House, a day-care center for children of immigrant parents, and low income housing for the elderly. "These projects," said Mary Lou Kownacki O.S.B. (the national coordinator of Pax Christi), "reflect our commitment to those who are the victims of the war economy."

The Benedictines have radicalized their traditional commitment to community. Their strong and explicit commitment to community life has been a major factor in attracting new members every year, including a significant number of transfers from other congregations. There was a palpable sense of pride among the members of this community and a sense of a common vision. It became apparent that their corporate commitment to peace had led many members to a much more critical sense of America and to a creative transformation of their own Benedictine tradition. The community seemed to reflect those values that its prioress, Joan Chittister, had described in a paper on the future of religious life:

> Those groups who survived the most cultural changes over long periods of time were those who, whatever the structures or rules, held tight to six values: a basic and important belief system, community and a sense of responsibility to one another, the renunciation of conflicting commitments outside the group, self-control, common ownership, and a willingness to sacrifice self for the sake of others.[4]

Joan Chittister and several other Benedictines have been involved in the "resourcement" of their tradition. They have begun to unlock the counter-cultural thrust of their tradition and relate it to contemporary concerns such as peace, feminism, and economic justice. The Benedictines' renewed commitment to common prayer and liturgy seemed important in sustaining an alternative vision to that of the empire. We were impressed that many members of the community referred to the Sunday eucharistic celebration as the high point of their week. The Benedictines of Erie have

a strong feminist commitment and are critical of many of the clerical structures in the church. However, the community has chosen
to look for new meaning in traditional symbols instead of manu-
facturing their own.

The monastery also had its artists and musicians and a marve-
lous potter by the name of Thomas. Like the community at Celo,
the Benedictine monastery in Erie seemed to exemplify the importance of an alternative that involved the transformation of every
dimension of life.

In reflecting on these two places, which we discovered at the
beginning and the end of our pilgrimage, I was struck by how
each integrated alternative was constructed from a different starting point. Celo began with an alternate economic basis which was
soon reflected in the other dimensions of the life of the community. The Benedictines of Erie began by reaffirming the value of
community and a corporate commitment and then engaged in
transforming other dimensions of their lives.

The experience of these two communities suggests that religious
congregations may differ as to which dimension of their life in the
present will break open the possibility of the future. In other words,
there may be different starting points for transformation, depending on a congregation's charism, history, or the gifts of its present
members. In any case, that starting point will open up the future
to the extent that it opens up the possibility of transformation in
all areas of life.

This pilgrimage provoked me to reflect further on how a radicalization of one dimension of religious life (ministry or community
or prayer) can lead to a radicalization of the other two dimensions.

A mission (a project, a ministry, an apostolate) that stretches us
to our limits will inevitably draw us to prayer and to one another.
The experience of moving from the too possible to the almost impossible tends to activate our sense of need for God and for others.
This need is not felt as acutely when we act within the realm of
what is possible. Even if we are very busy doing what is possible,
we tend to think that we can manage on our own if we just work
harder. The illusion of being able to manage begins to disappear
when you begin to associate with the powerless or confront the

powers that be. Works begin to seem almost impossible. The Sisters of Sion in Winnipeg, who live and work with the native people in the inner city, have come to such a realization. Reflecting on their more than eight years of experience there, they have written a letter about their growing need for community and prayer:

> ...Often we encounter our own inadequacy in the face of enormous social problems. We know our need to depend on others and on God as we constantly face our limitations. At the same time, we are called to action, to prayer and to work in a way which has empowered each of us....We have had to learn how to be here—in good part from the people who have more experience of suffering than we do. We have a deeper need for community than we had in other situations. It would be an impossible task alone. We have learned from the Spirit that we must pray, rest and play if we are to remain for the long struggle in love and hope.

I had some glimpse of the way radical action demands radical community and prayer when I was involved against the leaders of the nuclear industry. During a long forty-days-and-nights vigil outside a nuclear weapons plant in Toronto, in the coldest time of the year, I knew that my faithfulness could be sustained only with others and in prayer. We needed each other for the most basic reasons: to keep warm, to eat, to keep standing. And prayer, which felt almost impossible, never seemed more necessary.

Through my involvement with several congregations, I have noticed how apostolic groups tend to speak of their work as an area of promise for the future and to refer to prayer and community as more problematic. Before this pilgrimage, I would have concurred with that assessment. Now I wonder whether there is something problematic about apostolic work that does not call forth more authentic community and prayer. If we work only in the realm of the possible, then community and prayer seem more impossible and even unnecessary.

There is a second and related reason why a radicalization of mission will inevitably lead to a radicalization of prayer and community. This has to do with sustaining a vision for mission. Anyone who places himself or herself on the periphery of the empire soon begins to internalize some of the fear and violence of the powerless. The darkness that dwells in our own subconscious can be unleashed by prolonged involvement in the suffering of others. We may also project our own powerlessness and fear onto others, thus deepening the darkness of those who live on the margins of the empire. If we continually confront the powers-that-be in the empire, we may become like the very thing we are fighting against. For example, in working for institutional change, we may become as bureaucratic and impersonal as those who resist such change. When we enter into the circle of power and powerlessness, we can easily become more part of the problem than of the solution. This is true whether working for better housing, for curriculum changes, or for better nutrition for the elderly. Without a dream, our finest apostolic efforts can become a nightmare—for ourselves and others. If we are not sustained by a sense of what we are for, we will soon be defined by what we are against. If we are not animated by hope for the Kingdom, we will end up reinforcing the domination of the empire.

We are driven to prayer and community when we have engaged ourselves to the point where we experience our own limits and those of others. We need to pray in order to be with our own suffering and that of others. Otherwise, the darkness shall have dominion over us. We need to be with others who will sustain us in the faith that we, together with the outcasts of the empire, are really citizens of the Kingdom. When we hold each other to this vision of faith, we are more able to recognize that there is far more than fear and powerlessness in the peripheral places of this society. Bottom line: love, lived in hope.

It is also possible that a congregation may begin to open up its possibility for the future by radicalizing the call to community. A community may consciously begin to take those steps that will attune it to the call of the Spirit: through prayer, through a clarification of personal relationships, or through a process of liberation from the seductions of consumerism and the myths of the culture.[5] A community that begins to simplify its life and take time to reflect and encourages a depth of contemplation encompassing universal concern may become supple enough and strong enough to respond to the call of this hour.

I used to be puzzled by the many processes of congregational long-term planning that never seemed to move beyond the planning point. After this pilgrimage, I am a little less puzzled. The paralysis that grips many a planning process is not simply indicative of the inability of liberals to exercise some options that would exclude others. It could also be indicative of the level of shared faith in a community. Some communities feel genuinely unable to discern the direction of the Spirit in the options before them. They face the facts of their present situation more in fear than in trust. This paralyzing demon of fear will only be cast out as a community sounds the depths of its own faith—sounding the depths of the mystery of Love that releases its own truth and the power to follow that truth.

A community that radicalizes its commitment to live the gospel together may be more open to hear the radical call of the Kingdom in the midst of the empire. Many of us are culturally addicted enough to need a sustained counter-culture experience of a radical gospel community before our desire for radical service emerges. As long as community is lived merely on a functional level, we will remain more productive than prophetic in our service.

However, if we attempt to live community on a more than functional level, we soon experience the limitations of human community. If we live through and in these limitations, we may also be led to a more radical sense of prayer. I found some help in articulating this dynamic while I was on pilgrimage. The help came from Parker Palmer, a Quaker who was part of an effort to build "a new monastic community" at St. Benedict's Center in Madison, Wisconsin. Palmer, his wife, and family had come to Madison to live in community with some Benedictine sisters and Christians of other denominations. They were weaving their lives together by drawing on some of the Benedictine and Quaker traditions. Palmer told us that, in his opinion, these two traditions held greater resources for the building of community than did the

Protestant tradition—which offered more resources for action and service.

As I listened to Palmer reflect on his experiences, I realized how often I had not seen the darkness of community through to more radical prayer. He talked about how people usually deal with their disillusionment in community. Some retreat into isolation and individualism, and others remain in community but withdraw their hopes and enthusiasms from it. But the collapse of a romantic notion of community, he said, could also be an invitation to understand it as a *via negativa* to prayer.

> The primary spiritual function of community is to disillusion us about ourselves, remembering that "disillusionment" is a positive process in the spiritual life; it means losing our illusions so that we may come closer to reality. The human failures of community teach us to put our trust in God, where it belongs, and not in our own skills and charm. As we learn this lesson, the paradox ripens. In trusting in God we become more trustworthy to each other, more available for authentic community that is grounded in God's power and not our own.[6]

After my conversation with Palmer, I began to understand how those who have experienced not only the potential but also the poverty of community would be more ready for a radical engagement in action. The "disillusioned" person would be more likely to see through the illusions of empire, more likely to avoid the temptations of fabricating further illusions, more likely to desire the reality of the Kingdom. Community can be the starting place for a more radical love of God and of our neighbor.

These interwoven reflections also suggest that a congregation may begin to position itself for the future through a radicalization of its life of prayer, which in turn may lead to more radical forms of community and service.

Our pilgrimage led us to a group of women who live in the Carmelite monastery in Indianapolis. This community has become known for its work in translating the Psalter into inclusive language. They are now working on a translation that will include "liberating" language. The translation of the Psalter is much more than a grammatical exercise for them. It is an exercise of transformation wrought first in the daily process of praying the psalms together. Their radical commitment to silence seemed to have made them even more sensitive to the power of words to either deform or transform. Their contemplative way of life had moved them to a deeper sense of solidarity with all women and had moved them to undertake a work of liberation consistent with their lifestyle. There was an internal coherence between their option for contemplation, their commitment to community, and their decision to place themselves in solidarity with a group that often experiences itself on the periphery of the church and society.

Through our visits to these various places, we began to discover a strand of the Spirit that could be part of the process of reweaving religious life: a vital, alternative way of life involves an integration of all of the dimensions of life—including and especially the dimensions of prayer, community, and apostolate.

Lifelines

The Appalachian mountains in Kentucky were covered with a quilt of colors during our autumn pilgrimage. We drove through the mauve, russet, and amber trying to find the town of Nerinx. We missed it many times over, not realizing that the motherhouse of the Sisters of Loretto (our destination) was the village of Nerinx! We had to find it in the dark, directed only by the occasional passerby on the road.

In the morning, we wandered over to the edge of the motherhouse property in order to find Cedars of Peace, a colony of about twenty hermits. We had heard the stories of people who went here to live as hermits for a few months or a few years. As I looked up into the blue sky, I noticed a small electrical wire linking the various hermitages, passing up and over the trees and back to the motherhouse. One of the sisters explained that the hermits had decided to locate on the edge of the motherhouse property because it was far enough from the center of activity and yet near enough to provide a way of connecting with a source of electricity and a supply of water.

The sight of this small electrical wire gave me an insight into the kind of connection that made the "signs of the Spirit" on the side roads possible. The thin wire was a symbol of both the distance and the relationship necessary in the creation of new social and religious alternatives. The hermits at Cedars of Peace needed some distance from the motherhouse in order to develop their own way of life. Nevertheless, they could not be completely disconnected from the lifeline to an established institution.

This type of connection, distant but related, was evident in two other places we visited on our pilgrimage. The Christine Center for Meditation (Ya Ha Ashram) in Wisconsin is supported largely through the financial contributions of the Franciscan Sisters of Wheaton. This kind of institutional financial support is also true at Visitation House of Prayer (or "the Barn" as it is popularly known). The Barn is on the edge of the motherhouse property of the I.H.M. sisters of Monroe, Michigan. Both places were founded to create a space in which something new could happen. That space was created on the edge, but not outside of, more familiar territory.

A relationship between these small beginnings and an established congregation seems to have been crucial in the development of creative alternatives. On the most obvious level, it seems that the Cedars of Peace, the Christine Center, and the Barn would have foundered or, at least, not flourished, without the financial assistance of the congregation they were related to. On a deeper level, these alternatives seemed sustained by some relationship, some lifeline, to the charism of the congregation and the tradition of the church. The size and shape of that lifeline varied from place to place but it was always there. A certain distance from the institutional church or from aspects of the tradition was also always evident to a greater or lesser extent.

The connection to the Christian tradition manifested itself in various ways. In some places, there was a regular celebration of the liturgy and a recognizable place of Catholic worship. In other places, there were simply candles and icons and incense. Sometimes, the Scriptures formed the basis for prayer and reflection. At other times the Scriptures were one of several books that guided the prayer of the community. Some communities spent a great deal of time reflecting on contemporary church teachings, and in other communities that seemed less relevant. Some places of prayer drew heavily on the Western tradition, while others drew equally on the native and Eastern traditions.

A certain distance from the Christian tradition seemed to open up a space for some very creative forms of life, prayer, and action. The people were shaping their lives on a side road rather distant geographically from the centers of ecclesiastical interests and control. They spent a great deal of energy dealing with the latest directive from the chancery office, but they were not as caught up in the endless circle of disputes between liberals and conservatives in the church. It was not that the people on the side roads were unaware of what was happening in the mainstream church; they were simply more interested in something else. For them, the Christian tradition was a source of life, a resource, and they were engaged in the process of "resourcement," which John Coleman suggests is so crucial for the future of the church in America.

The distance from the institutional church provided the space in which to discover new meaning and vitality in the Christian tradition. It was a discovery that seemed beyond either liberalizing the tradition or conserving it. On the side roads, the conservative effort to control the tradition appeared less possible and the liberal desire to be free of this control, less necessary. The distance from the institutional church opened the possibility of creative fidelity to the tradition.

I recall the early morning prayer at the Christine Center for Meditation. We gathered in the large loft area of an old barn, unrolled our prayer mats, and turned to the rising sun. After forty-five minutes of physical exercises and breathing exercises, we gathered in a circle to listen to the gospel of the day. I had never gone through such a strenuous preparation for listening to the Word. These preparatory exercises would be viewed with scepticism by some who worship in the churches on the highways of America. On a side road in Wisconsin, it was more possible to discover a new meaning for the traditional ascetical practice of "remote preparation for prayer."

I also noticed that the "distance" of these counter-cultural places also provided them with a perspective from which to criticize aspects of the Christian tradition. From a distance, it seemed more possible to see which Christian practices had flourished because of the church's predominant position in the mainstream of society. It became easier to see through the theologies that had arisen from the church's adaptation to the powerful in this and other empires.

Nevertheless, these places remained connected, although critically, to the church and its tradition. This connection was one of the reasons for the longevity of the places we visited and why so many saw them as "signs of the Spirit." This connection with a long tradition of spirituality makes it more possible for these communities on the side roads to disconnect themselves from the values of the dominant culture. In my experience with some experimental groups, I noticed that when they became disconnected from the Christian tradition they have usually ended up forming an even stronger connection with the values of the dominant culture. The groups that started out with a radical intention gradually began to adopt the liberal or conservative ways of coping in the culture. Professing to be counter-cultural while practicing the beliefs of the empire, these groups soon collapse in a state of internal contradiction. I have watched, with some sadness, as a feminist group (which was formed as an alternative to the patriarchal church) soon became a merely liberal group fostering the self-development of the members. It had lost some basis for being truly counter-cultural. A total disconnection from the Christian tradition and its living reality leaves a group with a need to reconnect somewhere. And it is not difficult to make connections with the empire.

The political significance of an explicit connection with the Christian tradition has been noted by others in the peace movement. Secular activist Barbara Epstein has commented on the long-term resolve of those who draw energy from a religious tradition. "Christians in the direct action movement take personal responsibility very seriously. It is they who tend to take the greatest risks, both in terms of physical safety and of lengthy jail sentences."[7] In reflecting on the sustained radicalism of these groups, Epstein says that they "tend to be better able to articulate the large questions of meaning that drew them into the movement and sustain their political activity."[8] She remarks that Christians are often able to bring a historical perspective to radical peace-making that other groups do not.

> Many religious activists bring a historical perspective to the movement which others lack. It is not that others are without a sense of tradition, but the pagans, the witches, the anarchists have adopted their beliefs rather than growing up in them, and the traditions with which they identify lack the solid continuity of organized religion.[9]

Barbara Epstein's comments on the relationship between a rootedness in the Christian tradition and the radicalness of a political option describes the dynamic that characterizes the "signs of the Spirit" in the midst of the empire.

The Power of Attraction

I was not prepared for the sheer beauty of the places we visited on this pilgrimage. The Visitation House of Prayer in Monroe was centered around a barn that had been converted into a space beamed with beauty. At Celo, the simplicity of the buildings was so attuned to the natural surroundings that a sense of harmony filled the air. The works of art that graced the interior of the houses in Celo brought the integrity of creation home once again.

At the motherhouse of the Sisters of Loretto in Nerinx, we went to a liturgy during which we sang the music composed by Sr. Jean Marie Richardson S.L., one of the hermits at Cedars of Peace. There we also visited the studio of another sister of Loretto, Jeanne Dueber, who has been a sculptor for 18 years. Her abstract figures in wood and bronze reflect her attempt to achieve a "linear simplicity." Jeanne gathers her wood at Nerinx and then lives with it for two to eight years as it seasons.

Another surprising discovery awaited us at the motherhouse of

the Dominican Sisters in Adrian, Michigan. A small side building
has become the design studio (INAI) for two Dominican sisters
who are architects. They used their gifts throughout the United
States and Canada in the renovation of older religious institutions. The models in the studio reveal how these two women have
cleared away spaces within older buildings in order to give full
play to the natural light. Their alteration of interior spaces illus-
trated the kind of transformation taking place on many levels
along the side roads of America. The creation of a new physical
space often coincided with the creation of a space for new life.

The beauty we encountered on the side roads was not purchased at great financial expense; the quality of graceful integrity
arose more from an investment of spirit. It is a beauty rarely seen
in the expensive buildings on the highways of America, which are
often functional, bland, and even ugly—the constructions of a bar-
ren spirit.

There are beautiful places for beautiful people on the highways, but the cost of these aesthetic spaces is often paid for by
those who are forced to live and work in the ugliness of poverty.
Religious who have chosen to be in solidarity with those on the
periphery sometimes come to accept such ugliness as the inevitable consequence of poverty. I myself went through a phase of
assuming that justice work had to take place in the dreariest of
conditions. It wasn't real unless it appeared as drab as possible. It
may have been admirable but it certainly wasn't very attractive.
After this pilgrimage, I began to see that the lack of beauty in all
this had more to do with an impoverishment of spirit than with
the scarcity of economic resources.

Attractive. That is how I would describe the "signs of the Spirit" on the side roads. The beauty of these places was an expression of a centered and integrated way of life. Beauty flourishes
when there is an integrity of relationships between persons and
God and the world. When there is an appropriate relationship between things and persons, something lovely appears. The idols
manufactured through consumerism are ugly; the creations of human beings serve to dignify and delight. A tune can be played, a
color can be splashed, a dance can begin—even in the poorest of

circumstances. A beautiful room, for example, has nothing to do with the amount of furniture or the cost of decoration. It has to do with the way the room is arranged. People who have really rearranged their lives and ordered them along the lines of justice and love will shape their environment in a beautiful way.

However, beauty was not the only "sign of the Spirit." There was also a measure of charity, joy, peace, patience, benignity, goodness, and long-suffering (Gal. 5:22). These attractive qualities of life are often in short supply in the empire. People will go a long way to find them.

As we journeyed from place to place, we found that we were always asked about the other stops on our pilgrimage. People wanted to know what others were doing, how it was going. It was as if we were all engaged in a process of mutual encouragement. Those who lived along the side roads often felt that their efforts were small and fragile. At times, the effort of staking out an alternative space seemed daunting. They took heart in hearing news of others who were also going out to the frontier, the desert, or the periphery. Together, we found the courage to name the realities of the declining empire and the encouragement to live according to the vision of the Kingdom.

Before this pilgrimage, I would have used one of two mental maps to describe the situation of the American church at this time. I would have used a more traditional map to follow the lines of the pyramidal structure of the church, i.e., national offices, bishops, parishes. Or a more liberal map to trace the various networks of interests and concerns among Christians. Now I would describe North America as one vast desert space of a great thirsting for authentic religious meaning. A map of this desert space would have tiny dots here and there indicating the small oases (signs of the Spirit) where many pilgrims go to be refreshed. News travels fast and far about these oases. Pilgrims will travel hundreds of miles to get to these places—in search of something to sustain them on the journey.

This strand of attraction is significant in considering the possibility of reweaving religious life. It suggests a way of life that embodies the attractiveness of the Kingdom even in the midst of the empire.

A Certain Fiber

In reporting on my pilgrimage, I have noted at some length the counter-cultural quality of the signs of the Spirit in the midst of the empire. Yet, it must be said that these places were truly American, i.e., authentically enculturated. In creating an alternative to the empire, these communities drew not only on the Judaeo-Christian tradition but also on the counter-cultural tradition within America itself. Their resistance to the empire did not imply a rejection of all that is American. Indeed, there was a willing embrace of what was considered best in America.

I was intrigued by the pictures on the walls of the communities we visited. They were pictures of the martyrs, the holy ones and the wise ones of the church on the side roads of America. Almost all were pictures of Americans: Dorothy Day, Martin Luther King, Jr., the four women martyred in El Salvador.

Their pictures were displayed prominently in every place along the side road. The books of Thomas Merton, another American, seemed to have become a standard reference for these communities. There is a consensus of the faithful regarding those who are the spiritual inspirations of resistance to the empire. That inspiration draws some of its breath from the cultural atmosphere of the United States itself.

Another example from history may help us to understand this culturally grounded resistance to the dominant culture. One could understand the Benedictine monasteries which arose in the fifth and sixth centuries as counter-cultural communities formed in the time of the decline of the Roman empire. These communities resisted a pattern of decline by forming an integrated way of life that involved an alternative way of working, praying, and being together. The Benedictine rule also embodied a resistance to the clerical patterns that had taken shape after the Constantinian alliance of church and state. The resistance of these monasteries was thus twofold: against the patterns of decline in the church and in the empire. At the edge of a declining empire, early monasticism was a prophetic way of life, denouncing the evils of the empire and announcing the possibility of an alternative future for the culture and for the church.

However, although Benedict resisted the empire, he did not totally reject the culture that was Rome. He developed and transformed what he thought was best in Roman culture: a sense of just law and order. Benedictine monasteries would provide a bridge between the collapse of the Roman empire and the beginning of the Christian Middle Ages. (Unfortunately, the mediaeval period did not realize the Benedictine ideal of a network of Christian collective farms.)[10]

An alternative that does not draw on the best energies of its own culture will not even be recognized as meaningful. Within the United States and Canada, there are historical strands that can be drawn on in weaving an alternative to the empire. Our histories are not without a certain fiber.

Within the United States, the republican vision of the founders remains an alternative to the imperial illusions of the American empire. There are also what Robert Bellah calls "communities of memory" which can nourish a cultural alternative to the present patterns of liberal individualism in America.[11] He holds that there is an early tradition of individualism in America which, unlike the later forms of utilitarian or expressive individualism, emphasizes the development of the individual for the purpose of sharing with others.[12] In addition, there are many examples of persons and groups who consciously set out to resist the dominant political and economic patterns of periods in American history. Few American children graduate from high school without having heard about Henry David Thoreau's move to Walden Pond on a side road of America.

Canada's early history was shaped by communities of resistance. Against the vast and threatening forces of the north, the early settlers erected their little outposts of civilization. They learned how to survive the cruelties of winter through building communities of co-operation and consensus. This communal form of resistance took another, more political, shape after the American Revolution. For some, Canada itself became a place of resistance to the expanding power of America. Even though Canada has become an economic colony of the United States, there remains a thread of resistance to its imperial power. The history of Canada is full of stories of small groups of people who survive against the odds, who build something good together.

It seems clear that any attempt to reweave religious life in North America must draw on the strands of what is best in this culture. And there is much that is good. In both the United States and Canada, the tradition of democracy is strong and deep. In addition, the growing cultural insight into the equality of women is promising. These two cultural strands, the older strand of democracy and the newer one of feminism, may be transformed into strands of the Spirit in the reweaving of religious life.

Richard Rohr O.F.M. has written with great conviction about the gift of the American church being its honest search for authentic spiritual authority.

> The American Catholic is too independent, honest, and sensible to bow before ascribed and acquired authority which is not real authority. And what is real authority? Quite simply the ability to rightly name reality. In the religious realm, that is the ability to speak in the name of the Holy and the ability to transmit proven holiness to others. That lets no one off the hook. Leadership and membership both owe one another holiness. That is the full authority of the body of Christ.
>
> We American Catholics believe in and need authentic spiritual leadership. But we also believe that we are in this faith thing together. The way of consultation, dialogue, and humility must be the Christ witness that precedes any and all authoritative pronouncements....
>
> I believe the Catholic church in America has the gift and the potential to redeem the intuitive Catholic respect for authority, and to rediscover its base and power....I think we have the self-confidence to now recognize and support authoritative leadership even when it is not institutionalized...without either withdrawing or rebelling. That includes the baptismal based authority of lay women, lay men and religious communities.[13]

The No Name Places

In reflecting on this pilgrimage, I am struck by how many places were not suggested as "signs of the Spirit." No one, for example, suggested a charismatic renewal group, although this is a very significant reality in the North American church. This omission may have been due to the kind of person I consulted before the pilgrimage. It may also indicate that the charismatic movement is too fluid to be identified with any particular place. However, the question I asked did not automatically invite a specification of place.

I was also struck that no one mentioned some of the more ultra-conservative movements or centers, which are certainly counter-cultural in their own way (counter to the liberal drift of things). Again, this may have something to do with the characteristic interests of those I consulted. It may also indicate a conscious or subconscious attitude that these ultra-conservative places have more to do with consolidating the past than with opening up the future.

I was even more surprised that there was no suggestion of a place that could be called specifically feminist. This, in spite of the fact that many of the people I talked to would have called themselves feminists. I discussed this with Lucy Edlebeck O.P., who animates a women's resource center called Interweave in Milwaukee, Wisconsin. Her work in this center is notable in its attempt to reach out beyond the middle-class confines of feminist concerns to women who are poor or of various races. She wondered whether the omission of explicitly feminist places had to do with where the women's movement was at this stage of its development. It is still in its critical phase of defining itself against what has been, and has yet to enter fully into a more constructive and creative phrase. Perhaps it will simply take more time before feminism can move beyond the necessary rejection of past oppression to become an attractive and hopeful sign for the future. Given the long history of sexism, feminism deserves to take the time it needs.

However, it is worth noting that all of the places we visited were places of liberation for women. On the side roads, inclusion and equality seemed to flourish almost naturally. The liberation of women seemed to be an integral part of the overall attempt to create a space of liberation from the dominant patterns of the empire. Personal liberation was not separate from but rather related to social, economic, political, and religious liberation.

Nevertheless, these omissions were relative compared to all the other places that were not mentioned—not one school, not one parish, not one university, not one retreat house, not one hospital. And these are the places where most of the church's financial and personnel resources are invested, where most religious put all their time and energy.

What does this say? The question deepened for me when I recalled that most of the people I consulted, prior to the pilgrimage, worked in precisely these kinds of places. What does this say about what they feel they are doing with their lives? I have no answers, but I do think they are good questions. It is important to know which of the threads of these times are not yet strong enough or have become too thin to connect us with the future.

At the Nevada test site, in El Salvador, and on the side roads of America, I listened to stories that were really stories about God who is Creator, Redeemer, and Spirit among us. I heard about the beginning of a new chapter in the story God is writing with us about the church and religious life in these times.

"It was very early
on the first day of the week
and still dark
when Mary of Magdala
came to the tomb."
John 20:1

"I hope in thee for us."
Gabriel Marcel

"Hope (deep-grounded hope,
not those sporadic cries and promptings
wrung from us in extremity
that more resemble despair)
is a climate of the mind
and an organ of apprehension."
Thornton Wilder

"For years, he was searching for a language,
an image that would contain and convey
certain passionate convictions....
The light that finally flared in his soul
took this form:
a religious imagery of sacrifice."
Daniel Berrigan S.J.

CHAPTER FIVE

REWEAVING RELIGIOUS LIFE

Let me gather the threads of thought that have led us to this point. Religious life North America is disintegrating to the extent that it has internalized the patterns of decline in liberal capitalism. That disintegration, evident in every aspect of our lives, is symptomatic of the loss of a common and integrating vision. We are experiencing a crisis of meaning that will not be easily solved. This is our experience of the dark night, a time in which a former meaning of religious life has faded and a future vision has yet to come into focus. If we deny the reality of this dark night or attempt to escape from it too quickly, we may miss the call of this hour in North America. Our challenge is to learn how to be in this dark time in a way that opens the possibility of the future. I have suggested that we can position ourselves to recognize the revelation of the future by placing ourselves together in prayer, by placing ourselves on the periphery of the empire, and by going on pilgrimage together. In these places we may discover those strands of the Spirit that may be rewoven to form the fabric of religious life for the future.

In sum, I have been reflecting on *why* it is important to consider the reweaving of religious life and *where* that reweaving could begin to take place. I turn now to the questions of *when* the process of reweaving could or should begin, *how* it may be done, and by *whom.* My comments on these questions will be, of necessity, more limited and preliminary. I will try to thread my way between the extremes of either saying everything or saying nothing. Something, however limited, must be said about the realities involved in the process of beginning religious life anew. My hope is that these tentative reflections will at least encourage others to think about these questions, and possibly find different, better, answers.

BEGINNING SOONER RATHER THAN LATER

In the previous chapters, I have emphasized that the authentic reweaving of religious life cannot be done in haste. We need time to recognize the ties that bind us to the patterns of the empire and time to free ourselves from that bondage. We need time to allow our spirits to become clearer through a confrontation with the realities of these dark times. We need time to discover the signs of the Spirit which hold the promise of the future. This process of preparation cannot be cut short. To do so would be to risk fabricating some form of religious life that will not wear long or well.

Nevertheless, the process of reweaving must begin sooner than later. If my experience with various congregations in North America is any indication, the unraveling of religious life is well underway. As mentioned in Chapters Two and Four, more conservative groups are trying to stop this process of disintegration by retreating to some past pattern of religious life or by attempting to impose a pattern of order on the chaos of the present. More liberal groups are simply "treading water": they don't want to go back but they don't know where ahead is. I have discussed some of the reasons why these liberal and conservative efforts at coping with the present situation of religious life are doomed to failure.

There is another, more profound, reason why these attempts at coping will accelerate rather than retard the process of disintegration in religious life. This relates to the fact that these different forms of coping are really survival tactics. Corporate bodies may persist through such tactics but the soul of religious life will begin to shrivel when survival becomes the ultimate concern.[1] Religious life is a way of following Jesus Christ today or it is no way at all. And the way of Jesus is not the way of survival but the way of freely chosen sacrifice. Jesus did not treasure his life and hoard it; he gave it away—freely and fully. The meaning of his life was in the freedom of love. If we profess to live our lives according to the gospel and yet act as if survival was our ultimate concern, then we render our lives and the message of the gospel meaningless.

"Sacrifice" is not a popular word in a liberal culture. The reason for this, related to the limits of liberalism, is that sacrifice implies the willingness to go beyond one's self-interest for the sake of something greater, something more meaningful. The notion of sacrifice has also fallen into some disrepute among religious, particularly women. Understandably so. Sacrifices have, more often than not, been imposed on women in the church by a partriarchal hierarchy. These imposed sacrifices have left many women with a feeling of servility. Sacrificial living does not appear to be very liberating for many women at this time. There is a world of difference, however, between a sacrifice that is imposed and one that is freely chosen. If women are to be more than just survivors in the church, we need to find the freedom to choose to sacrifice ourselves for what we have discovered to be meaningful. If the women's movement is to be more than just a female version of liberalism, then we must resist the temptation to manufacture our own meaning and must risk discovering the meaning that moves through our experience and calls us beyond it.

To choose to survive is to choose not to die, but it is not automatically a choice to live.[2] There is a second choice involved in choosing to live. The choice for life demands sacrificing something in the present for the sake of the future. In the words of the gospel, those who choose to lose their life will find it. As I learned from people in El Salvador, those who are free to die are also free to live.

We cannot begin to reweave religious life merely to survive. Paradoxically, religious life will not survive by surviving. Reweaving is more than putting a patch on things. We can begin to reweave religious life when we are ready to sacrifice those ways in which our lives have become tied to the present. If we are not willing to make these sacrifices, the revitalization of religious life will be put off until later...and later. We will become content with the appearance of vitality.

"The Future Belongs to Those Who Have Nothing to Lose"
In a talk I heard in the early 1970s, Marxist philosopher Herbert Marcuse forcefully articulated the depth of sacrifice demanded by a new future. He described his search for "the revolutionary subject," for those people who would take the initiative for radical social change. He recalled how he had invested a great deal of hope in various marginal groups—people of color, students, women. However, he had found to his dismay that each of these groups ceased to be revolutionary when they became more accepted by mainstream society. Once these groups began to enjoy some of the benefits and perks of belonging to the system, they ceased to be agents of social change. Marcuse ended his talk still wistfully looking for "the revolutionary subject." While he could no longer identify any particular group with his hope for radical change, he did conclude that "the future belongs to those with nothing to lose."

Over the years, I have sometimes mused about how religious life could be the ideal school for revolutionary subjects. The way religious life is structured through the vows of poverty, chastity, and obedience could help us become people "with nothing to lose." The vows could take on a new meaning if they were understood as a way of freeing us for a future that would be more than a slight variation on the present. If we lived the vows with this radical intentionality we could begin the process of reweaving religious life sooner rather than later.

My experience, though, tells me the sad truth that we often have a great deal to lose; we have a great deal invested in the past and in the present. There are many things, many relationships, many projects, many roles and self-images we have invested ourselves in. Each person and each congregation has something to lose. The more we have to lose, the less likely we are to begin the process of reweaving religious life.

LOOSENING THE BONDS OF LIBERALISM

It is important for persons and communities to become more conscious of the particular investments in the past and present that prevent an investment in the future. The results of such a consideration would no doubt reflect the diversity of individual and communal histories. Nevertheless, it is generally true that most religious congregations in North America have a great deal invested in the liberal model of religious life. We have invested ourselves in this model as an alternative to the more traditional model of religious life that the Vatican threatens to impose on us. We have done this as the way of becoming more relevant to our culture. We have paid a price for this liberal model with our blood, sweat, tears, and time; it is the something we have "to lose."

Unfortunately, we are spending a great deal of energy to ensure that this liberal model of religious life survives. I have mentioned how liberal congregations have tended to make their statements of charism and mission vague enough so that all of the present members will feel comfortable within the corporate definition. Comfortable—but not challenged. Liberal congregations continue to survive by allowing greater diversity made possible through the vaguest of visions and the most minimal common commitments in the concrete. This may facilitate a greater sense of belonging but it weakens the sense of commitment, at least to the congregation and maybe even to the gospel.

Some of the most interesting conversations about the future of religious life take place late at night, in small groups, during conferences for those in leadership positions. I vividly recall participating in dark-to-dawn conversations in both the United States and Canada. These were the times when people felt freer to wonder out loud about the future of their congregations. Most were acutely aware that the future of their communities was in doubt. Most held some hope for the future in a few members of their congregation. In one conversation, someone asked, "Who do you think could make a new beginning in your congregation?" The interesting thing was that everyone there could almost immediately identify some "beginners" by name. The people named came from every age and interest group. They didn't fit into any particular category, yet their congregational leaders could easily identify something promising about them.

I must admit that I do not know of anyone involved in those late-night conversations who ever acted on his or her feelings about the future in the clear light of day. This is curious, given the fact that most of them were strong and capable leaders, good people. We kept on trying to hold the whole group together in whatever way we could. We tried to encourage new ventures within the congregation and tried to keep them in some ongoing relationship to the group as a whole. In the process, of course, the radical potential of any new venture was minimalized. The commitments to new ventures were tolerated only as long as they did not threaten the sense of belonging of the other members.

Why were these leaders of liberal congregations so unable or unwilling to free some of their members for a new and possibly different future? There are some very human reasons for this reluctance. Most people who serve as leaders in liberal groups were probably elected, at least in part, because of their roots in the shared history of a congregation and because of their care for the community as a whole. Once elected, they probably become even more concerned about the security of the elderly or sick members of the community. Such care and concern runs deep and long.

Yet, the reluctance to risk commitments to the future, which would threaten the sense of belonging in a group, also reveals the extent to which many of us have internalized the ideology of liberalism. We have made the unity of the congregation the highest, and often unquestioned, value. We have made the reconciliation of all differences the highest virtue of leadership. We can be satisfied when differences are minimalized by establishing a minimal sense of unity.

We have much to lose. In order to be free for the future, liberal religious have to be willing to sacrifice the already minimal unity of the congregation and the sense of belonging that that has created.

One might think liberal congregations would be open to every possibility for future. Yet, it seems as if they can be open to everything except what challenges the basic values of liberalism. Liberals can tolerate everything—except what calls into question the value of unlimited tolerance for diversity. Liberals practice an admirable openness to every option—except one that calls for a common vision that compels the sacrifice of individual commitments and interests for the sake of a common commitment.

Most liberals tend to think of themselves as progressive, seeing themselves in conflict with the traditional model of religious life or with the conservative elements in the church. In some ways, this conflict is important for the liberal sense of identity. The progressive quality of liberal religious life appears more clearly when the regressive character of the institutional church makes itself felt. This conflict with conservative elements (either within the church or within one's congregation) is real and often painful. However, it may also blind us to the significance of an emerging conflict within religious life: between the liberal and more radical models of religious life. Some radical groups, in Latin America and in North America, are beginning to see liberalism as the most serious obstacle in the way of serious change in the church or in the culture. Here is an assessment from *Latinamerica Press:*

> While it continues to be represented by an unbending remnant, the traditionalist church has been displaced and remains only a relic of the past. The real tension in the Latin American church today is between the modernizing and prophetic lines.
>
> In many essentials, the modernizing church continues to have far more in common with the traditionalist than with the prophetic church. Liturgical reforms, the updating of clerical dress and lifestyles and the appearance of a younger, more vigorous generation of leaders are all positive developments, but unless they mediate more profound changes they will represent little more than tardy adaptations to contemporary capitalist mores.[3]

This suggests that the liberal model of religious life, which tends to see itself as a progressive force within the structure of the church, can also become (consciously or subconsciously) involved in conserving the status quo of liberal capitalism. In general, liberals tend to be more critical of the church than of the culture of liberal capitalism.

The conflict between the liberal and more radical models of religious life often takes place within the same congregation. At a recent chapter of elections in a more liberal congregation, one of the candidates for superior general spoke to the group about how she would envision herself in that role:

> I would encourage, by every means available, a more radical expression of gospel values in our lives:
> - I would prefer us to live in low-income neighborhoods than professional-class neighborhoods.
> - I would prefer us to do pastoral ministry in a frontier diocese than in a resource-rich urban diocese.
> - I would sacrifice high-paying professional jobs in favor of those which further the cause of justice or meet the needs of the victims of injustice.
> - I would give a priority to radical gospel ministries over the staffing needs of our institutions.

After receiving the feedback of the chapter delegates, this person withdrew her name. She was clear that she could not pursue this agenda without doing violence to herself or to the group. The congregation respected her greatly, but the model of religious life she represented could be tolerated only as long as it was one of several options within the congregation. Her agenda was considered too radical—to pursue it the congregation would have had to make some difficult choices.

The dynamics and the significance of this kind of conflict have remained largely unarticulated. As a result, this conflict lacks some of the clear energy that arises from the painful, yet pointed, conflict between liberals and conservatives. One of the first steps in reweaving religious life would be to attempt to articulate and explore the point of the conflict between the liberal and radical models of religious life. If we do not surface this conflict more consciously, we will probably minimize it as a question of personality conflicts. The conflict will then lose its creative power in shaping the future of religious life.

There are radical elements within each liberal group. The conflict between the liberal and the more radical members takes place in fits and starts. Their differences are usually stated more in terms of style than of substance. The radicals criticize liberals for being wishy-washy about issues; the liberals criticize the radicals for being fanatical, rigid, or doctrinaire. This kind of criticism may be true on one level and yet unhelpful on another. There are doubtless psychological reasons why someone may be wishy-washy or fanatical or rigid or doctrinaire. These unhealthy psychological patterns should not automatically be conferred with social or ecclesial significance. Not everyone who says "radical, radical" is a liberal; not everyone who cries, "liberal, liberal" is a radical.

Still, these qualifications should not obscure the fact that there is an emerging, substantial conflict between the liberal and radical models of religious life. Within each of these models, there is a measure of sin and grace, possibilities and limitations. The basic difference between these two models appears related to the question of "boundaries." The boundaries in a liberal congregation are wider and looser than the more clearly drawn boundaries in a radical model. It is pointless to moralize about these two models, to classify one as good and the other as bad. The point is to try to discern which model holds open the promise of the future at this time in history. My reflections thus far lead me to conclude that the liberal model of religious life is disintegrating as surely as liberal capitalism is disintegrating in the West. The question now is whether this liberal model, through its own process of disintegration, can give birth to a new model (or new models) of religious life.

Creative Disintegration

Moments of cultural disintegration have always been significant in the development of new models of religious life. "Major turning points are likely to occur in religious life when both the church and secular culture are in the midst of major changes and when religious life itself is disoriented by upheaval."[4] These new models are often embodied in new religious communities that spring up in the gap between the past and future. A cultural crisis creates the need for a new constitutive meaning and a new religious response. As the Roman empire began to disintegrate, the new integrating vision of Benedictine monasticism was born. My pilgrimage to the side roads of America indicates that new religious communities are being born today in the midst of the disintegration of the American empire. Some of these communities will die on the vine, but some will flourish and bear fruit in due season.

What about existing religious congregations? Most studies indicate that, in a time of cultural disintegration, many congregations will die and some will just survive.[5] Yet, it is just possible that some congregations will give birth to new forms of religious life and to new communities.

Is it possible for liberal religious congregations to do anything more than either die with dignity or survive with effort? Is it possible to do anything more than tread water? If liberals do not want to go back, then possibly the only way to forge ahead would involve an even greater liberalization and disintegration. In this case, the choice would be for a creative disintegration, consciously chosen. This could be a meaningful choice. There is a world of difference between drifting into disintegration, sometimes destructively so, and consciously directing the process of disintegration. The unraveling of the liberal model of religious life is happening anyway. It may yet be possible to see unraveling through as part of the process of reweaving religious life.

Concretely, what could this mean? While hardly the final word, something can and must be said about this now. A further liberalization of religious life would mean encouraging an even greater pluralism than has already existed. There are probably many models of religious life within most liberal congregations. The differences between them has been minimized somewhat to sustain the unity of a congregation. As a result, there has been neither the energy nor the encouragement for these models to develop as genuine alternatives.

Radical Pluralism

A liberal congregation could encourage its members to form smaller groups, each committed to different apostolic projects (existing or new projects), to form groups committed to a particular lifestyle, or groups committed to a certain spirituality and form of prayer. In other words, these groups would be formed on the basis of some passionately shared commitment. In order for them to develop the genuine alternatives inherent in these various possibilities, they would need to have, at least initially, some distance from and yet some relationship to the original congregation. They would need the kind of small lifeline similar to those I saw during my pilgrimage to places that were signs of the Spirit.

One sister explained radical pluralism to me in more personal terms:

> I think of the motherhouse as giving birth to a wide variety of new beginnings. Like every true parent, the motherhouse needs to give these new offspring the freedom to grow and develop in unique ways. Some will turn out well and others won't—but they are all our children and loved.

Such a radical pluralism would indeed jeopardize the already minimal unity in a liberal congregation. However, it may just foster a deeper and more dynamically committed unity within the smaller groups. This unity would not be imposed from without (as the conservatives are wont to do) but freely chosen from within the group.

This more radical pluralism would breed its own form of chaos, but it could be meaningful chaos if it is chosen as a way of redirecting and re-energizing religious life for the sake of furthering the Reign of God. If the commitment to this radical pluralism was sustained for a period of time, then there would indeed be some movement in liberal religious congregations—and some of that movement would be "ahead," into the future.

This movement could begin to take shape in three ways.

1. Groups reformed around specific apostolic projects or concerns. Some of these may commit themselves to specific institu-

tions as a corporate apostolic project. They may discover together a new energy for transforming the direction of these institutions in the light of the realities of a declining empire. In the process, the members of these groups may discover the forms of community life and prayer appropriate for this institutional commitment.

Other apostolic groups may be formed in response to an urgent need that has emerged on the periphery of the empire. This need would create its own imperative for a style of community and prayer that would sustain this commitment.

2. Groups reformed around a certain lifestyle. With the collapse of the traditional model of a uniform community life, liberal congregations have evolved a wide variety of forms of community life, some in response to the demands of ministry and others in response to the personal needs of the members. There are small communities, clusters, support groups, loose networks of people living alone, inter-congregational communities, and intentional communities based on a commitment to certain values or projects. This diversity in community life is encouraged and tolerated to a point. However, there has been little encouragement to develop the spirituality appropriate for each particular lifestyle. There is a difference, for example, in the spirituality needed to live alone and the spirituality needed to live in a community involved in social resistance.

At this point, it is possible to foresee at least two significant developments arising from choosing a radical pluralism in community life: the fostering of the ministry of women in the church, and the forming of communities of social resistance.

The clusters, support groups, and networks of individuals within a congregation could be developed to the point where these people formed a network of women working in church ministry. Given the lack of support for women working in the church, this network could be of particular importance at this point in history. It would provide a base of support (personal, material, and spiritual) for women to minister within the wider church community. Belonging to such a network could sustain women in the difficult commitment entailed by church ministry during this time.

A radical pluralism would also encourage the development

of communities formed for the purpose of resisting the disintegrating patterns of the empire. These communities would be free to choose the maximum requirements for sustaining such a resistance. They could discover together the appropriate spirituality and the practical asceticism needed by such an option.

3. Communities reformed by a commitment to a particular form of spirituality. There are many spiritualities operating within liberal congregations at the present moment: Ignatian, Eastern, Carmelite, feminist, creationist, etc. Although this pluralism can be mutually enriching, it can also lead to a spiritual impoverishment. To commit oneself to living according to the deep dynamics of a particular spirituality is to find the roots from which to branch. A more radical pluralism in spiritualities would encourage the emergence of communities with a deeper and more dynamic spirituality. The forms of action emerging from this would be more energized and better directed.

These are some of the developments that could occur if liberal congregations chose a more radical pluralism. My descriptions are obviously incomplete and perhaps even inaccurate, but they may provide a "feel" for the possibilities that could be opened through the conscious choice for creative disintegration.

Here are five even more tentative reflections.

1. Through the process of radical pluralism, some groups may continue to be animated by the charism of the original congregation and may even bring new life and meaning to that charism. Other groups, however, may find the original charism fading as they become more distanced from the congregation from which they emerged. They may discover a new charism that constitutes them as a distinct group, or they may find themselves without a sense of charismatic purpose and may eventually disband.

2. In the dynamic I have described, the groups reformed from within a liberal congregation are initially related to the congregation through the "lifeline" of its tradition and charism. What would provide the "distance" necessary for this radical pluralism to develop into genuine alternatives for religious life? This is a most difficult question. My tentative conclusion is that these groups must be allowed a significant measure of independence

from the original congregation in the areas of government, finance, and formation. There can be no radical pluralism if everyone falls under the same model of government, no genuine pluralism if groups do not have the responsibility of directing their finances according to their own priorities.

I have already alluded to the frustration of trying to form new members for all the options available within a liberal congregation. The truth is that new members are probably initially attracted by one of the models of religious life, or by some of the people living that model. Their incorporation process is confusing, to say the least, when they find themselves introduced to another model of religious life. It would seem more authentic to have new members incorporated into the model they are attracted to. Allowing for greater pluralism in formation would make it possible to be shaped in different ways: one type of formation for those attracted to one model, another type for those called to another model. To make formation more focused would move it beyond belonging to the stage of commitment.

The decision to encourage a radical pluralism in government, finances, and formation would indicate whether a congregation is creatively disintegrating or merely disintegrating.

3. The choice for a more radical pluralism presumes that liberal congregations who attempt to author the future more consciously have the authority to do so. Yet, this authority is being challenged by the Vatican. There is no end in sight to the ongoing struggle between the Vatican attempt to order religious life and the desire of religious to shape their own response to the problems and possibilities they face. For some liberal congregations, the struggle with the Vatican has seemed increasingly meaningless. However, this struggle could take on new meaning if liberals saw it as more than merely a struggle to survive. It could become a struggle willingly undertaken for the sake of discovering and creating new meaning in religious life.

4. In a situation of more radical pluralism, we could anticipate that some of the more traditional distinctions between the apostolic, monastic, and contemplative forms of life would begin to break down. It is possible, for example, that communities formed

as integrated alternatives to the disintegrating patterns of the empire would combine some elements of all these three forms of life—but in a new way. My pilgrimage seemed to reveal the importance of arriving at such an integration, regardless of the point from which the process of integration began.

5. All the options generated through this radical pluralism seem to be potentially open to the membership of lay people, clergy, or members of various congregations. Many liberal congregations have already initiated programs for including associates or co-members. The quality of these efforts at inclusion varies from congregation to congregation depending, perhaps, on the particularities of the program or the congregation. However, every congregation I know of that is engaged in such programs wants to discern its direction in an ongoing way. What could be the basis for this discernment? Some of the previous reflections on the limits of liberalism (Chapters One to Three) may be helpful in this regard. Do these programs foster a sense of belonging or do they encourage deeper commitment? Are they a survival tactic for a congregation, or do they foster meaningful sacrifice on the part of all concerned? Are they ways of coping with the present or ways of risking the future?

These are some of the considerations involved in loosening the bonds of liberalism, some of the ways that indicate *how* the reweaving of religious life might begin. The question remains as to *who* will do the reweaving.

A PROPHETIC MOMENT

Who are the discoverers of a new meaning for religious life in these times? Who will help to create a post-liberal model of religious life? These questions, in one way or another, are being posed at an increasing number of conferences in North America and elsewhere. One of the most significant articulators of this kind of questioning is Gerald Arbuckle S.M. He makes a persuasive case for the importance of "refounding," or prophetic, persons at this point in the history of most religious congregations. His character-ization of these persons is provocative:

> Seized by the Spirit, they yearn to adapt the inner heart of the founding experience to the new pastoral/spiritual needs of today. And they invite others to join them in their task. They have a faith-stubbornness and a humility that comes from an awareness of their own failings and their utter dependence on God, that ultimately carry them through the inevitable periods of opposition, rejection, even marginaliza-tion within their own congregations.[6]

What Arbuckle refers to as refounders, I have referred to as the reweavers of religious life. His description of these people (their human, psychological, and spiritual gifts) makes a very important contribution to moving the question of the future of religious life forward, but I differ slightly from his emphasis on the qualities needed and on the significance of refounding individuals.

The one thing necessary is commitment. This is not a personali-ty trait; it cannot be measured on a Myers-Briggs test or located on the Enneagram. The quality and gift of commitment can be found quite unexpectedly in the most diverse kinds of people. Who is willing to see religious life through to the future? There are ways of discovering these people in whom commitment is really operative.

Let me give an example from my involvement in the peace movement. One of the biggest problems in the peace movement is what has been called "the flake factor," i.e., people who drift in and out of meetings, who may or may not show up for an action. Recognizing this problem, a group of us decided to form a new peace group that would, we hoped, provide a basis for solid and committed action. Quite unexpectedly, we happened upon a way of filtering out the uncommitted. We set the meeting for 6:00 A.M. once a week. Attendance at the meeting was the only requirement for membership in the group. We soon discovered that those who were willing to make the sacrifice to attend at this early hour were also the ones who could be counted on to see an action through.

In religious communities today, we need some similar concrete way of discovering who is willing to make sacrifices and commitments to see religious life through.

I also sense that the refounding, or reweaving, of religious life will be less dependent on certain individuals and more likely to arise from within a small group. There are three reasons why I say this. The first is based on my experience in helping to start new ventures; the second reason has to do with my understanding of the prophetic call in the church; the third flows from my reflections on the interactive quality of grace, charism, and power. I will expand on each of these reasons.

1. I have had a few small experiences of participating in the creation of something new in the church. In each case, something new was born in the process of a small group gathering over an extended period of time to discuss a problem or need. Through our interaction with each other we discovered the energy and the courage to begin something new.

Catholic New Times, for example, was founded when three of us started talking about some of the problems associated with the official Catholic newspaper. We widened the conversation to include about ten other people and we continued to meet together over a period of a year. In the course of that time together, our ideas about the problem were clarified and we started to examine possible solutions. We didn't begin these conversations with the clear idea of starting an alternative Catholic newspaper. It was only in the course of these conversations that the idea became clearer and our commitment to it deepened. Many of us crossed the Rubicon sometime during that year of discussion. A few did not.

As I reflect on this process, I think it was significant that many of us in that group were women. We simply assumed that it was better to work together co-operatively. Some people have called this little newspaper "prophetic" but I know that no single person founded this newspaper. We became prophetic together at a certain moment and something prophetic was born in the church.

2. This experience has led me to study the prophetic experience in the Scriptures more deeply. Before I began this study, I shared

the stereotypical view of the prophet as a beardy-weirdy with eyes blazing and voice booming: "Thus saith the Lord." Yet, I soon saw that this caricature hardly fit the descriptions of the prophets of old. They came in every shade and stripe; they were poets and people with a very proper upbringing, the pugnacious and the petulent. All of them were quite different, but alike in that they were chosen from among the people, for the people, with a certain message for a specific situation. The fact that prophets are defined as such because of their call to address a specific situation led me to the rather shocking realization that prophets are not born that way but become so when they are called. Being prophetic is a temporary assignment. In other words, it is not a personality trait some are born with and others are not. It is a way of being, called for by a certain situation for the sake of the community as a whole.

I found this consideration helpful in the difficult, ongoing task of discerning between true and false prophets. We can begin to sense the falseness of a so-called prophet when he or she acts as if they have something to say about every situation or issue. And we must begin to question our own sense of who is a prophet if we deny the prophetic truth a person has spoken just because we know that what they say about another situation or issue rings false.

As I read the reports about the prophets in the Scriptures, I saw that their coverage lasted only as long as their message was significant for the community. We do not read about them before or after the situation that called them forth and defined them. No one possesses the gift of prophecy forever. It possesses us— sometimes, somewhere.

These considerations led me to believe that each one of us has a prophetic moment—sometimes, somewhere. Yet, I noticed how easily I (we) continued to cling to the illusion of the prophets being a special race of people, even when the evidence of Scripture refused to support such an illusion. Why? Perhaps it is a way of protecting ourselves, a way of denying the possibility that we too may have one or two or three prophetic moments in our lives. As long as we can believe in the illusion that prophets are few and far between, we can relax for the rest of the time—which is most of the time. As long as we continue to imagine that the prophets today are "special" people, we don't need to face ourselves or the situations in which we find ourselves.

All of which leads me to believe that just as each of us has "prophetic moments," so too a group of people may have a prophetic moment.

Most congregations refer to their founder as a prophetic person. Perhaps it would be more accurate to say that they had a prophetic moment in which they received a gift of the Spirit for the whole church. They did not possess this gift, it possessed them. We who belong to the congregation they started do not possess this charism any more than they possessed it. It possesses us sometimes, in some places. We start to think of a charism as something possessed or passed on only when we think of charism as a *thing*. Yet, a grace, or charism, is not a *thing*; it is an energy, a dynamism, a power that cannot be contained or possessed. It is relational. It becomes real and actual only when it is acted on, believed in, and shared.

3. I imagine grace, or charism, as a power actualized in the in-betweens of life: between persons and between persons and God. In the political realm, power is what arises from the interaction of people. "While strength is the natural quality of an individual seen in isolation, power springs up between [people] when they act together and vanishes the moment they disperse."[7] In this sense, power is not something some people have much of and others have little of. Power is an energy that grows through the sharing of power.

To imagine grace or charism or power in interactional terms is also to acknowledge that there are certain requirements for its actualization. People must be together, and they must be together with God. They must interact with God and with each other, and they must do so over a period of time. Unfortunately, the conditions for this kind of interaction are not usually present at most chapters or decision-making meetings in congregations. This kind of interaction is much easier in a smaller group over an extended period of time. Smaller groups are not necessarily weaker;

through dynamic interaction, they may have the potential for greater charismatic energy and power.

It is interesting to reread the founding stories of congregations from this interactional perspective. One begins to wonder how many of the official stories that emphasize the singular role of the founder could be reinterpreted to give more emphasis to the significance of the interaction of a small group in the founding moment of a congregation.[8]

With apologies to Carmelite historians, I want to draw out a small example of the interaction involved in the beginnings of the Carmelite reform. This story in no way negates the importance of Teresa of Avila in the reform of Carmel, but it does suggest some of the conditions under which new movements in religious life flourish. This new reading may encourage all of us to reread the story of our founding moment in order to come to a deeper understanding of the process of refounding, or reweaving, religious life in our times.

In 1560, Teresa was living in the large and rather liberal Convent of the Incarnation in Avila, Spain. In the evenings, she would gather with a small group of friends and admirers in the cell she shared with two young nieces, Beatriz and Maria Cepeda y Ocampo. The women in this small group would laugh and talk as they worked on their embroidery. One September evening, the talk turned to the early hermits of Mount Carmel. One of the nieces exclaimed how wonderful it would be to return to this simple and austere way of life. Others in the group took up the idea enthusiastically. (The niece later admitted that she hadn't been totally serious). However, another woman in the group offered to help finance the new venture. Teresa was drawn into this interaction.

Teresa smiled and listened to the others' eager talk. The idea of starting a convent for Discalced Carmelites where she and other like-minded nuns could live quietly according to the primitive Rule had been at the back of her mind for some time. But she had not given the matter much serious thought....The discussion ended with general agreement that they would commend the matter fervently to God in their prayers.[9]

A few days later, Teresa received a vision, or locution, in which the Lord commanded her to undertake this project. The rest is history. After a time of discernment and of intense struggle with those opposed to this reform effort, Teresa and a small group of nuns moved out of the Convent of the Incarnation to begin their radical alternative at the little convent of St. Joseph's.

This story gives us some inkling of how and with whom the reweaving of religious life might begin. It could begin by people talking together, being together, and then dreaming together. This could happen in a Carmelite convent, on the periphery of the empire, or even in the heart of the empire. The amazing grace is the grace of beginning anew. This grace is even more amazing in a time of cultural decline, in a world growing old and worn. There is also a grace to continue what has begun—to see a new vision through from the moment of its conception to its birth into reality.

SINGING THE SONG OF THE LORD
IN A STRANGE LAND

This could be a prophetic moment for religious life in North America. In responding to the call of this hour we can refer back to the scriptural stories of the response of the prophets during the exile inaugurated by the fall of Jerusalem in 587 B.C.E. The whole world of meaning associated with Jerusalem had disintegrated and the people were taken into captivity in the empire of Babylon. Three prophets arose to speak to the people at different moments in their captivity.

Jeremiah wept and lamented over the destruction of Jerusalem. He refused to deny what had happened or his people's participation in their own downfall. "He envisioned the death of a culture, a society, a tradition. He watched his world dying and he felt pain. What pained him even more was the failure of his contemporaries to notice, to care, to acknowledge, or to admit."[10]

Ezekiel, a younger contemporary of Jeremiah, recalled the radical transcendence of God and the divine power that would enable the people to do what they could not otherwise do for themselves. "A new heart I will give you, and a new spirit I will put within you; and I will take out of your flesh the heart of stone and give you a heart of flesh."

Second Isaiah (Isaiah 40–55) was called to speak to the people after they had been in the empire of Babylon for some time. They had started to adapt to the patterns of the empire and their memories of Jerusalem had grown dim. The Babylonian empire was itself entering into decline because of the rising power of Persia. These patterns of decline were being internalized by the people of Israel. Second Isaiah arose to evoke the memory of Jerusalem for those who had lost hope in the future, who had invested everything in their present state of exile. By recalling the memory of Jerusalem through the most beautiful poetic images, he was able to liberate the desire for an alternative future. This "future-giving memory is the main thing an established empire has to fear."[11] These three prophets exemplify three ways of being in a time of decline.

We who live in a disintegrating empire today are summoned at prophetic moments to *criticize* the patterns of decline within our culture and within ourselves, to *contemplate* the holiness of God in the midst of these dark times, and to evoke the *creative* desire in one another for a meaningful alternative for the future.

PROMISING THE FUTURE

The image of weaving or reweaving helps us to name the mysterious dynamic that enters into the process of shaping the future of religious life. We can engage in this activity even in the absence of any clear design or pattern to follow. We can begin—now.

We can shuttle back and forth between acting and praying and reflecting. At each moment, there is a further revelation that requires a further response and decision in order for the next step to be revealed. Reweaving religious life involves a commitment to this process; it involves promising to be there. It is through our promises that the promise of the future opens up for us. We do not predict or produce the future, we promise it.

How can we promise our lives in religious congregations today? We can promise our very selves because God has promised to be with us, to see things through with us. On Sinai God revealed God to be *ehyah asher ahyeh*. While this is often translated in the Hellenic words, "I am who am," it is more properly translated from the Hebrew as "I shall be there as there I shall be."[12] God promises to be present unconditionally in every moment but not in a way that can be anticipated. God promises to be there for us without saying how, or where, or when.

We do not know exactly how the process of reweaving religious life will unfold or when or where it will take place or with whom. Still, we can promise each other to see religious life through. We can promise to be there as there we shall be.

MEDITATION FOR A THREADBARE MOMENT

We face the empty loom.
It looms large before us
revealing a threadbare moment,
what has come apart at the seams.
Empty space. Dark time. Dark night.

The holy ones tell us
this is the space and time
in which God becomes
more than our god.

A space of not knowing,
a space beyond feeling.
A time not of weaving
but of being woven—
knit together in God's womb.
A space without meaning
in-between past and future,
in-between what is no longer there
and what is not yet here.
Neither here nor there.

Dark night of our times.
 Auschwitz. Hiroshima. Spaces,
 places emptied of people.
 Empty space of the world
 where the social fabric is frayed
 where only small threads
 of human mercy remain.

Difficult to see through.
 Dark night of our lives.

Religious lives
once filled with tensile truth
now stretched and taut
between past and future
neither here nor there.

Empty space of our lives.
We fill the void
projects and projections,
the pious and politically correct—
a fabric of vanishing threads.
We try to fabricate a future
manufacture meaning.
Fabrications aren't suited
to the life of faith
don't wear well.

Dark Night.
    Diminishment of numbers
    dimming of vision
    deadening of desire.
    An unraveling
    of the seams of our Spirit
    in a once seamless fabric.

    Darkness over the deep, empty space.

As in the beginning...
    A Spirit creating
    darkness and light
    void and vision.

As in the beginning...
    when there was neither here nor there
    when it was all in-between
    a space and time emptied
    of all but God.

And now we, like God, are beginners,
    beginning in nothingness
    believing that there is meaning
    in this dark time in-between.
    Believing that there is meaning
    without knowing what it is.
    Naming what is meaningless.
    Knowing the difference between
    meaning and meaninglessness.
    Understanding that meaning
    cannot be manufactured
    can only be discovered.

How do we discover the meaning of this moment?
    Perhaps not how but where.
    Where are the places, the spaces,
    to position ourselves for the future?
    Where should we place ourselves
    so the future may present itself?

We must place ourselves together
    in prayer, on the periphery,
    on pilgrimage.

Placing ourselves together in prayer:
    Visions find their first voice
    at the deepest level of our lives
    deeper than the conscious or
    self-conscious levels of our lives.
    In that space where
    we are who we truly are
    where we are of God,
    with God and for God
    where our lives are threaded with others
    in a seamless garment of Spirit.

    In this space visions are born.

In the in-between of our prayer
beyond isolation,
beyond superficial togetherness
let us dwell in silence
together—to wait, to listen.
Let us nourish this prayer
with the symbols and stories of
our outrageous faith.
Let us read the Scriptures together
letting the words form
in the silence of our being
letting the words shape
the word we have to speak together.
Let us wait in the hope
of co-authoring a new chapter.
Let us hold ourselves
in readiness for a vision.

Placing ourselves together on the periphery.
We position ourselves for the future
by taking our place
with those on the periphery
of the empire
with peripheral people
who know in their bones
that something is disintegrating.
Peripheral people
the ones whose future is most denied
by the lack of social vision.
They bear witness to the lie
of the empire. They cannot cope.
Inside the periphery of power
feeling neither very powerful
nor totally powerless
we will be tempted to cope
to keep on keeping on.
Outside the periphery of power

we will feel the hunger and thirst
for a different future.

Religious life always begins
on the periphery of power.
Founding people, now as then,
feel their hearts stretched
by some group, some need,
peripheral in their time.
What is peripheral becomes
central in their lives.
A founding moment:
when being centered in God
coincides with being pulled
to the periphery.

Placing ourselves on pilgrimage.
There is a long tradition
of going on pilgrimage
to holy places, holy spaces.
Now as then
we need to journey
to the places which hold
promise for the future.
We need to see, to touch
some small sign
that the future is real.

Where are those spaces?
People know.
We have only to ask.
Where have you seen life?
Where are the strands of the Spirit?
Where do you go to find God?
Where are the signs of justice and peace?
People know.
We must become pilgrims

for a while,
at least once in our lives
displaced people
dislocated, delighted, disturbed
by the signs of holiness in our land.
Such dislocation may lead
to a new sense of vocation
perhaps back to where we came from
but with a longer, lighter vision.

The holy places
small promises of the future
small beginnings
As in the beginning...
small creations, very good.

We face the empty loom
the loom without
is the loom within.
The Spirit weaves
with invisible threads
drawing us beyond
to one another, to the future.

As in the beginning
is now and ever shall be
world without end. Amen.

NOTES

INTRODUCTION

1. For a condensed consideration of the liberal model of religious life see my "Beyond the Liberal Model of Religious Life," in *The Way*, Supplement 65 (Summer 1989), pp. 40-53.

2. Cf. my "Exercising Theology in the Canadian Context," in *Faith That Transforms: Essays in Honor of Gregory Baum*, eds. Mary Jo Leddy N.D.S. and Mary Ann Hinsdale I.H.M. (Mahwah, N.J.: Paulist Press, 1987), pp.127–134.

3. Sandra Schneiders I.H.M., *New Wine, New Wineskins* (Mahwah, N.J.: Paulist Press, 1988) has rightly observed that the theology of contemporary religious life would benefit from more reflections based on the experience of women in religious life.

CHAPTER ONE

1. Cf. John Coleman S.J., *Towards an American Strategic Theology* (Mahwah, N.J.: Paulist Press, 1982), p. 155-165.

2. It is interesting to note that a film with such a startling title was made in Quebec, a French-speaking colony within the colony that is Canada. In one way, one could say that it is filmed from the edge of empire. In another way, one should point out that its angle of vision is that of the new emerging class of the information elite in a large metropolitan center (Montreal). From both perspectives, the film presents insights into the heart of the empire.

3. Hannah Arendt, "Home to Roost" in S.B. Warner (ed.), *The American Experiment* (Boston: Houghton Mifflin, 1976), pp. 64-65. This address originally appeared in *The New York Review of Books* (26 June 1975), pp. 3-6. For Arendt's study of the American revolution, see *On Revolution* (New York: Viking Press, 1963).

4. Peter Schmeisser, "Is America in Decline?" in *The New York Times Magazine* (17 April, 1988), pp. 24–26,66–68, 96. More recent articles still support this perspective: David S. Broder, "The Waning Days of Washington," *The Washington Post Weekly Edition* (Feb. 26—March 4, 1990. Broder Quotes Clark Clifford as saying (p. 9): "We reveled in the fact that we were the capital of the world. But it's drifted away now. We are beset,

instead, by questions about whether we are the murder capital of the country." See also Michael Oreskes, "Poll Detects Erosion of Positive Attitudes Toward Japan Among Americans," in *The New York Times* (February 6, 1990). Oreskes comments (p. 87) on a poll which shows "Americans made it clear that the highly visible Japanese investments here are feeding an anxiety that they are losing control of their own country and culture. Furthermore, the collapse of the Soviet bloc has freed them from their fears of Communism and allowed them to turn their anxieties toward what they see as their own nation's slipping economic strength."

5. Schmeisser, p. 24.

6. Paul Kennedy, *The Rise and Fall of the Great Powers* (New York: Random House, 1987), p. 527.

7. *Ibid.*, p. 533.

8. Robert Nisbet, *The Present Age: Progress and Anarchy in Modern America* (New York: Harper & Row, 1988), p. 39.

9. Walter Russell Mead, *Mortal Splendor: The American Empire in Transition* (Boston: Houghton Mifflin Company, 1987), p. 213.

10. Walter Russell Mead, "On the Road to Ruin," in *Harper's* (March 1990), p. 59.

11. Garry Wills, "What Happened?" in *Time* (9 March 1987), p. 40. This article was written as the Iran-Contra scandal was beginning to surface.

12. As quoted by Fergus M. Bordewich, "Colorado's Thriving Cults," in *The New York Times Magazine* (1 May 1988), p. 43.

13. Goethe, quoted by Robert Nisbet, p. 39.

14. Daniel J. Boorstin, *The Image: A Guide to Pseudo Events in America* (New York: Atheneum, 1987), p. 239.

15. Jim Wallis, "A Wolf in Sheep's Clothing," in *Sojourners* (20 Mary 1986), p. 19.

16. Walter Russell Mead, *Mortal Splendor*, p. 179.

17. For a clear and concise presentation of the liberal model, see Joe Holland and Peter Henriot S.J., *Social Analysis: Linking Faith and Justice* (Washington, D.C.: Center of Concern, 1980), especially pp. 14-15.

18. Cf. Ron Graham, *One-Eyed Kings: Promise and Illusion in Canadian Politics* (Toronto: Totem Books, Collins Publishers, 1987), pp. 14-15. "The United States began as a classic liberal culture, with its values and myths

in the individual and decentralized power, and it has more or less remained a classic liberal culture. But English Canada began as a conservative liberal culture, applied that way of looking at power to progressive goals, and developed into a radical liberal culture."

19. Walter Russell Mead, p. 34.

20. Joe Holland, "The Spiritual Crisis of Modern Culture" (Washington, D.C.: Center of Concern Monograph of address to Network Seminar, Summer 1983), p. 3.

21. Robert N. Bellah, et al., *Habits of the Heart; Individualism and Commitment in American Life* (New York: Harper & Row, 1985), p. 277.

22. *Ibid.*, p. 284.

23. David R. Gergen, "Avoiding the Great 'S' Word'," in *U.S. News & World Report* (29 February 1988), p. 76.

24. Walter Russell Mead, p. 272.

25. For an excellent study of the political context of Augustine's writings, see R.A. Markus, *Saeculum: History and Society in the Thought of St. Augustine* (Cambridge: Cambridge University Press, 1970). See also the insightful work of Jean-Marc Laporte S.J., *Patience and Power: Grace for the First World* (Mahwah, N.J.: Paulist Press, 1987), pp. 149–170. Laporte sees Augustine as a theologian who developed a theology of grace for a dying age.

26. For a more detailed discussion of the methodological questions involved in the process of reflecting on events in one's own time, see Mary Jo Leddy, "The Event of the Holocaust and the Philosophical Reflections of Hannah Arendt" (University of Toronto Doctoral Dissertation, 1980).

27. Alasdair MacIntyre, *After Virtue* (Notre Dame: University of Notre Dame Press, 1981), p. 244.

28. *Ibid.*, p. 245.

29. *Ibid.*, p. 245.

CHAPTER TWO

1. For a thorough presentation of the situation of the church in Quebec, see Daniel Donovan, "The Historical Context of North American

Theology: The Canadian Story," in *Proceedings of the Catholic Theology Society of America*, volume 41 (1986).

2. John Coleman, S.J., *Towards an American Strategic Theology*, p. 157.

3. *Ibid.*, p. 158.

4. Vaclav Havel, "The Chance That Will Not Return," in *U.S. News & World Report* (26 February 1990), p. 30.

5. John Kavanaugh S.J., *Following Christ in a Consumer Society* (Maryknoll, N.Y.: Orbis Books, 1981), p. 25.

6. Cf. Alvin Toffler, *Future Shock* (New York: Random House, 1970), pp. 238-322. For an insightful analysis of the corrosive effects of consumerism on the traditional middle-class value of self-denial, see Barbara Ehrenreich, *Fear of Falling: The Inner Life of the Middle Class* (New York: Pantheon Books, 1989).

7. Robert Bellah, et al., *Habits of the Heart*, 1985, pp. 142–163.

8. I owe the distinction between "belonging" and "commitment" to Reginald Bibby, *Fragmented Gods: The Poverty and Potential of Religion in Canada* (Toronto: Irwin Publishing, 1987). Bibby makes the point that Catholics in Canada are not so much "dropping out" of church but "dropping in."

9. Michael Crosby O.F.M. Cap., "Transforming Religious Life." Talk given to the National Association of Formation Directors of Canada (Ottawa: Canadian Religious Conference audiocassettes, set of 10).

10. Michael Crosby, "Transforming Religious Life." Crosby is here relying on Alasdair MacIntyre's discussion of bureaucratic individualism in *After Virtue*, pp. 22–34.

11. Mary Jo Leddy, "Here We Don't Believe in Idols—We See Them: An Interview with Jon Sobrino," in *Catholic New Times* (5 February 1989), p. 12.

12. Jon Sobrino, *The True Church and the Poor* (Maryknoll, N.Y.: Orbis Books, 1984), p. 319.

13. *Ibid.*

14. Jon Sobrino, p. 324.

15. *Ibid.*

16. Cf. Lawrence Cada, et al., *Shaping the Coming Age of Religious Life* (Worcester, Mass.: Seabury Press/The Marianists of Ohio, 1985), pp. 51–89.

17. *Ibid.*, p. 58.

18. *Ibid.*

19. Gerald A. Arbuckle S.M., *Out of Chaos: Refounding Religious Congregations* (Mahwah, N.J.: Paulist Press, 1988), p. 82.

20. *Ibid.*

Chapter Three

1. Cf. Paul Ricoeur, *History and Truth* (Evanston: Northwestern University Press, 1965). See also his introduction to *The Symbolism of Evil* (New York: Harper & Row, 1967), pp. 3–24 and Gregory Baum, *Religion and Alienation* (Mahwah, N.J.: Paulist Press, 1975), pp 238-266.

2. Cf. John of the Cross, *The Dark Night* (Book 1) in Kieran Kavanaugh O.C.D. and Otilio Rodriguez O.C.D. (eds.), *The Collected Works of John of the Cross* (Washington, D.C.: ICS Publications, Institute of Carmelite Studies, 1973), pp. 297-329.

3. Constance FitzGerald O.C.D., "Impasse and Dark Night," in Joann Wolski Conn (ed.), *Women's Spirituality* (Mahwah, N.J.: Paulist Press, 1986), p. 292.

4. *Ibid.*, p. 296.

5. *Ibid.*, p. 294.

6. Cf. Bernard Lonergan, on constitutive meaning in *Method in Theology*, pp. 57–101.

7. Victor Frankl, *The Will to Meaning* (New York: New American Library, 1969), p. 35. I am grateful to Fr. Tom McKillop for pointing out the significance of Frankl's reflections on meaning.

8. *Ibid.*, p. 127.

9. Cf. Mary Jo Leddy, "Between Destruction and Creation," in *Elie Wiesel: Between Memory and Hope* (ed. Carol Rittner R.S.M.) (Irvington, N.Y.: New York University Press, 1990).

10. Thomas Merton, *Conjectures of a Guilty Bystander* (New York: Doubleday, 1966), p. 142.

11. John Coleman S.J., *Towards an American Strategic Theology*, p. 158.

12. Thomas Merton, *Disputed Questions* (New York: Farrar, Straus and Cudahy, 1960), p. 160.

13. A book that probes the middle-class experience of powerlessness is written by Paul G. King, Kent Maynard, David O. Woodyard, *Risking Liberation: Middle Class Powerlessness and Social Heroism* (Atlanta: John Knox Press, 1988).

14. Jon Sobrino S.J., *The True Church and the Poor*, p. 324.

15. Leonardo Boff, *God's Witnesses in the Heart of the World* (Chicago: Claretian Center for Resources in Spirituality, 1981), p. 73.

16. Cf. John S. Dunne's notion of "passing over" in *A Search for God in Time and Memory* (New York: Macmillan, 1969), p. ix.

17. Cf. Rudolf Otto, *The Idea of the Holy* (New York: Oxford University Press, 1958).

CHAPTER FOUR

1. Cf. Emil Fackenheim's notion of "root experiences" in his *God's Presence in History* (New York: Harper Torchbooks, 1970), pp. 8-14.

2. Cf. Mary Jo Leddy, "Resisting Illusions: Spirituality for a Desert Time," in *Catholic New Times* (31 May 1987), p. 7.

3. Cf. Mary Jo Leddy, "And Death Shall Have No Dominion: Reflections from El Salvador" in *Catholic New Times* (5 February 1989), p. 13. Also reprinted as "Children in El Salvador," in *National Catholic Reporter* (17 March 1989), p. 28.

4. Joan Chittister O.S.B., *Women, Ministry and the Church* (Mahwah, N.J.: Paulist Press, 1983), p. 35.

5. Cf. Duane Elgin, *Voluntary Simplicity* (New York: William Morrow, 1981), p. 68. "The relative lack of community support was mentioned by many persons as being important in their adoption and degree of experimentation in alternative ways of life."

6. Parker Palmer, Newletter of St. Benedict's Center, Spring 1987.

7. Barbara Epstein, "The Politics of Prefigurative Community: the

Non-violent Direction Action Movement," in *Reshaping the U.S. Left* (eds. Mike Davis and Michael Sprinker), (London, Verso Press, 1988), p. 82. For a related study of new social movements see Carl Boggs, *Social Movements and Political Power* (Philadelphia: Temple University Press, 1986).

8. Barbara Epstein, p. 82.

9. *Ibid.*, p. 83.

10. Cf. Walter Dirks, "The Monks' Response," in *Concilium* vol. 97 (New York: Seabury Press, 1974), p. 13.

11. Cf. Robert Bellah, *Habits of the Heart*, pp. 152-155.

12. *Ibid.*, pp. 28–34.

13, Richard Rohr O.F.M., "The Future of the North American Church," in *Radical Grace* vol. 2, no. 1 (January-February 1989), p. 2. Rohr also notes, p. 10, the shadow side of this gift: "The North American Catholic church... is more American than Catholic, more individualistic than communitarian, more anti-authoritarian than really authoritative itself, more psychological that radically Gospel, more into the freedom of choice than the real and disciplined freedom of the children of God."

CHAPTER FIVE

1. My criticism of mere survival is confined to its dynamic within normal circumstances. However, there are some (extreme) situations in which survival is the final form of human freedom. Cf. Mary Jo Leddy, "The Event of the Holocaust and the Philosophical Reflections of Hannah Arendt" (University of Toronto Doctoral dissertation, 1980), pp. 282-283.

2. I am indebted to Anne Wilson Schaef for this insight.

3. David J. Molineaux, "Traditionalists, Modernizers, and Prophets," in *Latinamerica Press* (1 September 1983), pp. 5–6.

4. Lawrence Cada, et al., *Shaping the Coming Age of Religious Life*, p. 47.

5. Cf. Lawrence Cada, et al., "The Life Cycle of a Religious Community," pp. 51–76.

6. Gerald Arbuckle, *Out of Chaos*, p. 111.

7. Hannah Arendt, *The Human Condition* (Garden City, New York: Doubleday, 1959), p. 179.

8. For a slightly different presentation of this perspective, see Bernard J. Lee S.M., "A Socio-Historical Theology of Charism," in *Review for Religious* (Jan./Feb. 1989, Volume 48 Number 1), pp. 124–135.

9. Stephen Clissold, *St. Teresa of Avila* (New York: Seabury Press, 1982), pp. 70–71.

10. Walter Brueggemann, *Hopeful Imagination: Prophetic Voices in Exile* (Philadelphia: Fortress Press, 1986), p. 32.

11. *Ibid.*, p. 114.

12. Cf. Martin Buber, *Moses* (New York: Harper Torchbooks, 1958), pp. 51–52.

SELECTED BIBLIOGRAPHY

Arbuckle, Gerald A. *Out of Chaos: Refounding Religious Congregations*. Mahwah, N.J.: Paulist Press, 1988.

Bibby, Reginald. *Fragmented Gods: The Poverty and Potential of Religion in Canada*. Toronto: Irwin Publishing, 1987.

Bellah, Robert N., et al. *Habits of the Heart: Individualism and Commitment in American Life*. New York: Harper & Row, 1985.

Chittister, Joan. *Women, Ministry and the Church*. Mahwah, N.J.: Paulist Press, 1983.

Coleman, John. *Towards an American Strategic Theology*. Mahwah, N.J.: Paulist Press, 1982.

Conn, Joann Wolski (ed.). *Women's Spirituality*. Mahwah, N.J.: Paulist Press, 1986.

Ehrenreich, Barbara. *Fear of Falling: The Inner Life of the Middle Class*. New York: Pantheon Books, 1989.

Farley, Margaret A. *Personal Commitments*. San Francisco: Harper & Row, 1986.

Holland, Joe, and Peter Henriot. *Social Analysis: Linking Faith and Justice*. Washington, D.C.: Center of Concern, 1980.

Kavanaugh, John. *Following Christ in a Consumer Society*. Maryknoll, N.Y.: Orbis Books, 1981.

Mead, Walter Russell. *Mortal Splendour: The American Empire in Transition*. Boston: Houghton Mifflin, 1987.

Plaskow, Judith, and Carol P. Christ. *Weaving the Visions: Patterns in Feminist Spirituality*. San Francisco: Harper & Row, 1989.